# Sheba

# Sheba

From Hell to Happiness
Another dog rescue from the author
Of the bestselling 'Sasha'

*Brian L Porter*

# Introduction

Anyone who has read my earlier dog rescue story, Sasha, will perhaps remember a chapter being devoted to her best friend, Sheba. Such has been the reaction to that one chapter that I felt it only appropriate to tell Sheba's story in full, as many readers have asked me to. It was Sheba who, as our first ever Staffordshire Bull Terrier, began our love for the breed, so often maligned and misunderstood.

Sheba certainly experienced a harsh and brutal introduction to life in the human world, as the following story reveals. I freely admit that we made some mistakes along the way, especially in the early days of her time with us, but in mitigation I have to say we had no experience of dealing with a dog that had been so badly abused by the dog fighting fraternity. Thankfully, we learned from our mistakes as the following narrative will reveal.

Some of what follows may be upsetting and quite horrifying to some readers, but I make no apologies for telling the truth. This is Sheba's story, after all, and all rescue dogs have a tale to tell. So, without further ado, here is Sheba's tale…

# The Bait Dog

By Mick Byrne

*I died today*
*alone and scared*
*I cried for my humans*
*they never heard*

*They used to love me*
*or so I was told*
*now I lay lonely*
*lifeless and cold*

*I was not ready*
*to meet my fate*
*I forgive you my humans*
*for dogs do not hate*

The following work is by reader, Linda Lindsay, who wrote this after reading *Sasha*

# An ode to Sasha

By Linda Lindsay

*Abandoned in a gutter, so afraid and all alone,*
*Lay a precious angel, no one to call her own.*
*A kindly doggie warden ventured down the street that day,*
*And found this little puppy, almost dead just where she lay.*
*She took her to the centre, where dogs both lost and found,*
*Stay awhile and wait to see if owners can be found.*
*They wrapped her up in blankets, to keep her nice and warm,*
*They loved her back to health again, and kept her safe from harm.*
*Then there came two callers, who'd both been there before,*
*And rescued several doggies, who weren't wanted any more.*
*'Hi Juliet and Brian, come on in and say hello,*
*There's something I must show you; come and look before you go.*
*Just inside my office, there's someone you should meet,*
*There, inside the little box, the one beneath my seat'.*
*The Porters went towards the box, to have a little peep*
*And saw the little puppy, all curled up and fast asleep.*
*They heard about her story, and how she'd almost died,*
*About the love and kindness, that she had been denied.*
*It only took a moment, the Porters fell in love,*
*This tiny little creature, was sent from up above.*
*The puppy was so beautiful, from her tail up to her nose,*
*They saw in her an angel, wrapped up in Staffies clothes.*
*They simply had to have her, take care of all her needs*
*A look that passed between them said, the little pup agreed*
*Her little tail was wagging; a new home on the way*

*A very special friendship was forged upon that day.*
*The other doggies welcomed her, to her forever home,*
*Filled with love and kindness, and folks to call their own.*
*They called their puppy Sasha, she settled in so fast,*
*They knew this bond between them, was always going to last.*
*Then one day an accident, caught them unawares,*
*Little Sasha broke her leg, through falling down the stairs.*
*No sooner had they fixed it, she tried to jump a gate,*
*And though they tried to stop her, they knew it was too late.*
*The poorly leg was broken, their baby girl in pain,*
*But thankfully the surgeon, repaired it once again.*

*Then sickness came to Sasha, an ailment they can't cure*
*Pills and potions every day, poor Sasha must endure*
*No matter she's an Epi-Dog, despite the bumpy ride,*
*Her tail just keeps on wagging, she takes it in her stride.*

# A Short Glossary, Mainly for U.S. Readers

**UK - USA**

Lead - Leash
Garden - Yard
Dry food - Kibble

# Contents

*This book is dedicated to all dog rescuers, rescue dogs, and those who adopt and care for them, wherever in the world they may be.*

## Chapter 1

# One Cold Christmas Holiday…

It had been a very cold winter already, and we weren't yet into January. It was that week between Christmas and New Year, ten Christmases ago, when the world seems a strange, surreal place as we slowly recovered from the festivities of Christmas and lumbered almost sleepily towards the revelry of New Year's Eve. Whether by coincidence or design, I really can't remember, but on the 29th day of that very cold December, with snow that had fallen a couple of days too late to call it a white Christmas lying on the ground, and with nothing better planned for the day, my wife suggested a visit to our local Dog Pound. I'd earlier bought a very large box of chocolates as a gift for the staff at the pound, from where we'd adopted a number of our family of rescue dogs in the past. It seemed the least we could do to say a small 'thank you' to the girls who worked there, doing their best to try to make their often frightened and scarred residents feel as comfortable as possible, given the circumstances in which they had to work.

The accommodations at the pound weren't luxurious by any standards, but at least the dogs held there were sheltered, fed and watered, and safe from harm, and the owners of the pound operated a strict 'no kill' policy at that time. If a dog couldn't be rehomed in a reasonable period of time, they would often contact the specific breed rescue society who would collect the dog and take it to be rehomed through their own organisations.

So, wrapped up against the cold, my wife and I, accompanied by our two girls, aged seven and eight and both in junior school, piled into the car and set off on the fourteen mile journey to the pound with our present neatly wrapped and decorated with ribbon and bow. On arriving at the pound, we parked in an almost deserted car park. Obviously, with the post-Christmas sales in full flow, looking for a rescue dog to adopt was a pretty low priority for the majority of the local population.

The girls on duty were pleased to see us as always and expressed surprise and gratitude that we'd thought to visit them with a present. One of the girls, who we knew quite well after numerous visits to the pound, informed us that since Christmas Eve, they'd received over two hundred dogs into their care, a staggering number of innocent, unwanted souls. We found it hard to believe that so many people could heartlessly 'dispose' of family pets in this way. As we were told, although some of the dogs had been handed in by their owners for various reasons, the vast majority had simply been cast out by their owners, some having been found and handed in by members of the public, with most having been picked up and delivered to the pound by the dog warden service.

Though we hadn't gone there that day with the intention of adding to our family of rescue dogs, (at that time I think we had eleven in our home), we were encouraged by our friend Lisa to take a tour of the facility. She explained that due to the numbers received, they'd had to set up 'overflow' accommodation, using outbuildings and even part of the stables that formed part of the property. So, off we went, and within a minute of leaving reception we were being assaulted by dozens of pairs of pleading eyes and wagging tails, all virtually pleading to be taken out of their pens and given a new home. Some were less active then others, lethargic and often cowering towards the back of their pens, obvious victims of cruelty or some form of abuse. It's almost impossible to resist the appeal of some of those dogs and I'll never understand how some people can visit such establishments and leave empty-handed, saying they couldn't find one they liked.

Anyway, we continued our tour, and after leaving the regular kennel accommodation behind we entered the overspill areas, the barn and stable areas, where the staff had done a great job in erecting dozens of secure but temporary living areas. We could hardly bear the heartbreaking sights of so many dogs, abandoned and unwanted over the biggest holiday period of the year.

"It's not been much of a Christmas for these poor babies has it?" I said to my wife who nodded in agreement, a lump in her throat preventing her from making a proper reply. As we entered a small extension to the stable area we saw a small pen in the corner, set slightly apart from the others. We made our way to view the inhabitant of that lonely corner but were unprepared for the sight that greeted us as we looked into it. Having already viewed terriers of all descriptions, hounds of varying sizes and colours, and many cross breeds of indeterminate parentage both my wife and I caught our breath at what we now saw.

A heat lamp hung suspended from the ceiling, positioned directly above a small, shrivelled almost hairless dog, curled tightly in a foetal position, shivering or trembling, or perhaps both. A few wisps of fur led us to think she probably originally had either a dark brown or brindle coat, but we couldn't be sure.

Juliet grabbed my arm in shock, her gesture enough to convey her thoughts, much the same as mine: *How could anyone let a dog get into such a state?*

Juliet found her voice and spoke softly, trying her best not to scare the little dog, who also had numerous red sores and wheals on its body, an obvious case of serious abuse. Perhaps worst of all was the bright red ligature mark round its neck, looking sore and raw. In addition, we could see virtually every bone in the dog's body. We were staring at a living skeleton!

"Hello baby," Juliet said. "Who could have done this to you?"

The dog didn't look up, and continued to lie in its bed, curled up under the warmth of the lamp. The girls at the pound had obviously done all they could to make the dog comfortable with a bed lined with extra blankets for warmth.

"It's bloody criminal," I said, my anger at the dog's treatment for a few seconds overriding my sympathy for its plight.

We were unable to stop our girls from peering into the pen and though they tried not to cry, I could see tears forming in their eyes as they took in the sight of this poor dog.

"Can you tell what breed it is?" Juliet asked me, quietly.

"I'm not sure. It's hard to tell, but at a guess, I'd say it's a little staffy," I replied.

"It looks close to death's door," my wife said, choking back her own tears at this terrible sight, this symbol of man's inhumanity towards an innocent living creature. "I want to ask Lisa about it."

I nodded in agreement. The girls volunteered to stay with the dog to 'keep it company' as Juliet and I made our way back to the reception office.

Lisa smiled as we walked back into the warmth of reception. "Bet you've found something you like, haven't you?" she said with a knowing look in her eyes.

"Maybe," Juliet replied. "What can you tell us about the little dog in the stables, the one under the heat lamp?"

"Oh, that one. She's a little Staffy. One of the wardens brought her in three weeks ago. If you think she looks bad now, you should have seen her then. She was in a hell of a state. We honestly thought she wouldn't make it and the vet wanted to put her to sleep, but she lifted her head and looked up at us and... well, something made us decide to do what we could to try and save her. It was coming up to Christmas after all. So, the vet did what he could to treat her injuries and her skin condition and though she's made some progress, I don't think she'll make it in the long run."

"But what on earth happened to her?" I asked.

"That's quite a story too. Seems the warden's office received an anonymous phone call one day, telling them a dog had been thrown on a rubbish tip, I can't tell you where, and that the caller thought it might still be alive. A dog warden went and found the dog, exactly as the caller described, and loaded her into her van and brought her here. Both the warden and the vet realised right away the dog had been badly abused. The lack of fur on her body indicates she's been used as bait to train fighting dogs. They shave the poor dogs, to make it easier for the fighters to grab hold of their skin."

This was actually the first time either Juliet or I had learned anything about the world of dog fighting and I'm sure our faces must both have reflected the horror we felt at what we being told. After a pause for breath, Lisa continued her narrative.

"Our vet has been treating her since she arrived but there's not a lot more we can do. Her wounds are healing, but very slowly because of her poor overall condition. She's clearly been starved and the ligature marks round her neck are so deep it's obvious she's spent her life tied up while the fighters were trained to attack her. Poor dog has had no real life at all. From her size, we're guessing she was either stolen or bred for fighting but turned out to be an undersized runt so they used her as a bait dog instead."

"So, what's going to happen to her?" I asked, knowing full well what was in Juliet's mind.

"The vet thinks she's so weak, it's unlikely she'll live long," Lisa replied. "Funny thing is, when she does lift her head and look up at you, she does her best to wag her tail and be friendly. Like every dog we see, she's looking for a little bit of love."

"It's just awful that people do things like that and get away with it," Juliet commented.

"Not awful, just plain criminal," I said.

Lisa seemed to be thinking for a minute before she said, much to our surprise.

"Look, we know how you feel about dogs, and you've already got a houseful at home, but…" she paused.

"But what?" I asked.

"Well…maybe, if the boss agrees, and if you're willing, you could maybe take her home and try and give her the love she needs for however long she's got left."

"Please, go and ask her," Juliet said. "We'll take her, no problem."

Lisa disappeared and returned two minutes later with Kay, owner of the kennels, who confirmed the offer Lisa had made to us.

Lisa led us back to the stable where the girls were still patiently waiting for us, talking gently to the little dog. Lisa opened the gate and walked in to the pen, bent down and began stroking the dog, who lifted her head up and, sure enough, her tail began to wag, slowly at first, then with a little more gusto when Lisa picked her up and passed her into Juliet's arms. Juliet immediately began talking softly to our new and unexpected rescuedog, and Lisa reached down and took a blanket from the dog's bed and wrapped it around the little waif to help protect her from the cold as we walked across the yard to the office.

At reception, I was ready to fill out the necessary adoption papers and pay the usual fee for the dog but Kay held up her hand and told me they didn't want a penny for her.

"She's not exactly what people usually leave here with and she probably won't live very long. You two are marvellous for wanting to take her on and give her some loving care and affection. I doubt she's had one day of loving care in her life. Just take her home and do what you can for her. We'll do the basic adoption papers to comply with the legalities, but there'll be no fee for this little girl. You're doing us a favour by taking her."

A few minutes later, paperwork complete, and wrapped in a blanket we kept in the car at all times for our dogs, I carried our new rescue carefully in my arms and we gently loaded the little dog into our car, talking softly and reassuringly to her as we laid her on the large dog cushion that filled the large storage area in the rear of the estate car. As I closed the tailgate she looked at me and something seemed to spark in her mind and her tail wagged, just a little, as if she knew she was being rescued and going to a new home.

I drove slowly on the journey home, and the girls, who were quite small and could just see over the back seat, through the dog grille, reported that the little girl was sitting up and seemed far more alert and animated than she'd appeared in the pound. As we headed for home, we held a discussion about a name for the latest addition to our rescue family.

"Poor thing deserves a really good name, something proud and noble," I said. "Something to make up for the bad times she's suffered."

"I agree," Juliet concurred and between us we reeled off various names that might be appropriate for her, with numerous suggestions coming from the girls in the back seat.

Nearing home, I'm not sure after all this time whether it was me or Juliet who thought of it, but one of us suggested the name 'Sheba' as in the Queen of Sheba, reputed to have been one of the most beautiful women of her time, and usually known simply as 'Sheba' and even though the children were too young to understand the significance of the name they agreed it was a nice name for the little dog. We quickly agreed it would be a great name for her, so as we pulled up outside our home the decision had been made. Henceforth, the poor bedraggled and mightily abused, almost hairless little Staffy would be known as Sheba!

# Chapter 2

# A Bloody Tail

Peering through the rear window, we could see that Sheba was actually standing up with her tail wagging in the back of the car. Obviously, the journey had in some way reinvigorated her and perhaps, we thought, somehow she knows we are helping her.

I lifted the tailgate slowly and carefully, not wanting to scare her and the first thing we saw as the tailgate swung fully open was…blood! It was everywhere, on the large dog bed she'd been sitting on, the inside of the windows, the interior body of the car, I really mean everywhere. It looked as if someone had literally sprayed blood all over the inside of the car.

"Bloody hell," I swore.

"Where has all that come from?" Juliet gasped in shock. Both girls turned away in horror, not wanting to look at the right crimson streaks of blood that plastered the car. Juliet quickly picked Sheba up, looking for some injury that we didn't know about. It was me who suddenly noticed that as Sheba lay cradled in my wife's arms, her tail was wagging furiously and blood was spraying out from her tail, splashing onto my coat and the rear of the car and onto the street.

"It's her tail," I exclaimed and as Juliet held on to the little dog, I quickly ran into the house and returned a minute later with two of the 'dog towels' we used for cleaning up our dogs after walks in the rain or wet conditions. Juliet continued holding on to her as I first did my best to wipe her tail to get rid of the worst of the blood and then wrapped the tail in the other towel so we could get her into the house and examine her tail properly.

Taking Sheba through the back door and into the utility room, Juliet placed the little dog on the floor and we immediately noticed she had trouble standing up properly. Poor little girl's legs were very weak and she was holding her front legs at a strange angle as though she couldn't straighten them up properly, giving her a strange, frog-like appearance when she attempted to sit.

Juliet began doing her best to clean up Sheba's bleeding tail as I came to a quick conclusion.

"I think she must have been feeling happy and she somehow knew we being kind to her, and she wagged her tail so much in the back of the car, she spray-painted the inside of the luggage compartment for us!"

We had to see the funny side of the situation, even though it looked as though we may have a serious problem regarding her tail, one that would require veterinary treatment. The big problem was, it was Saturday afternoon and our vet practice closed at noon on Saturday, so there was nothing we could do until Monday. It would be up to us to stem the flow of blood and do our best to stop Sheba from redecorating the house once we allowed her into the kitchen. Our other dogs already knew she was there as they could see through the bars of the baby gate we used to separate the utility room from the kitchen. We could see a number of inquisitive canine faces peering at us through the gate, and the odd thing was, not one of the dogs barked as they usually would on seeing a new dog on the premises. When we thought about it later, we concluded that somehow, they must have sensed that the new dog was frightened and injured and they simply stood and observed the activity as we worked on Sheba's tail.

We possessed a powder that we kept in case of minor injuries to our dogs, that was intended to stop bleeding from minor wounds and scratches. Whatever was wrong with Sheba's tail was clearly not what we would have described as 'minor'; but it was the best we could do for her at that time.

Poor Sheba was trembling with fright and having trouble staying on her feet as Juliet did her best to keep her calm and stem the bleeding. In the meantime I had a phone call to make. I dialled the number for the Dog Pound and was fortunate when Lisa answered, just the person I wanted to speak to.

"Lisa," I said, "we just got home and the back of the car was full of blood from Sheba's tail when we opened up to take her out."

"Oh, heck, I forgot to mention that," she replied. "It slipped my mind as it wasn't something that happened much while she was here, as she spent most of the time curled up in a ball in her bed. We did see small amounts of blood now and then but our vet took a look and said he hoped it would heal up in time. He thinks the people who owned her starved her so much the poor little one had tried to stay alive by twisting round and attempting to eat her own tail. She must have felt so good in the back of your car that the wounds opened up and sprayed blood everywhere. I'm so sorry I forgot to tell you about it but I honestly thought it had almost healed up."

"Don't worry about it," I replied. "We'll do our best for now and I'll take her to our vet first thing on Monday. The car will clean up alright. Sheba's more important than a few bloodstains."

"I love the name you've given her," Lisa said. "I hope you can manage okay until you can get her to a vet."

"We'll be fine, honestly, Lisa. We wanted her to have a really posh name, something proud and noble, and Sheba seemed an obvious choice. Anyway, I just wanted to check with you to find out if you knew about the problem and you've cleared that up. I'd better go and help Juliet. We've still got to introduce her to our other dogs once we've stemmed the bleeding."

"Good luck with the introduction. I hope your other dogs accept her into the pack without any trouble."

"I'm sure they will, Lisa. Thanks again."

Sheba's tail gradually ceased its constant drip, drip, drip of blood and Juliet eventually brought away a tissue that bore no sign of blood. She cleaned the tail once more with a medicated wet-wipe and stood up, leaving Sheba to get her bearings for a minute.

"What about letting the others say hello?" I asked, as the other dogs weren't used to us coming home and not immediately letting them out into the garden.

Juliet agreed we should let the others come in to see Sheba, a couple at a time. We were aware of the fact that she could be fearful of the others, especially as her life so far had consisted of her being constantly attacked by other dogs in her role as a bait dog. How would she react to the rest of our pack? There was only one way to find out.

Much to our surprise, although she appeared nervous at first and very unsteady on her legs, Sheba readily accepted the 'dog style' greetings from our other dogs, all of whom were both people and dog-friendly. They each took it in turns to sniff the newcomer, a couple even touched noses with her and every one gave her a tail wag before leaving her alone as another pack member took their turn at 'exploring' this new addition. Juliet and I were quite moved by their behaviour over those few minutes. It was almost as if, through some silent method of communication, they knew of Sheba's previous treatment, that she wasn't well, and needed affection above all else. They definitely gave her a gentle and warm welcome into our home and Sheba eventually overcame her initial nervousness and began to wag her tail.

"Oh, I hope it isn't going to start bleeding again," Juliet said quietly, as though saying it too loud might bring on the bleeding again. For now though, no blood appeared and we hoped Sheba might follow one or two of the others into the garden to check out her new surroundings, but she seemed content to stay indoors for the moment. Perhaps, once she felt a little more confident on her legs, she might try to walk a little and go to the toilet outside. For now, patience was the main thing. We'd give her time to settle in slowly and assess what we needed to do to make her comfortable. She certainly looked a lot brighter and more alert than she had at the pound.

"Maybe she was depressed and felt alone in that pen," I observed. "Being here with us and the dogs might be what she needs to perk her spirits up."

"I know," said my wife. "I was just afraid she might turn on the others, you know, as she's been used to bait fighting dogs."

"I know what you mean. We need to find out what we can about how she's likely to have been treated, poor little dog, and what we can do to rehabilitate her properly."

"And what are we going to do about her tail?" Juliet asked.

"First thing, Monday morning, I'm taking her to the vets. I'll get them to check her over completely too and see what they think her chances are."

By now, the other dogs were simply coming and going as they usually do, in and out of the house and garden. They all seemed to virtually ignore Sheba, leaving her in peace and allowing her space and time to get used to her new surroundings. Juliet and I decided to leave Sheba in the utility room and we quietly walked away and into the kitchen, where Juliet put the kettle on to make us a coffee each. The children asked what was happening, having had the sense to stay in their rooms for the first, vitally important minutes of the newcomer's introduction to our home. They knew the drill, having welcomed others to our home in the previous couple of years.

Whether it was the children's voices, or the fact she suddenly realised she was on her own in the utility room, I can't say for sure, but we suddenly saw a little head appear in the doorway, followed by the rest of Sheba's horribly scarred and sore-covered body. As her tail came into view, we saw it was wagging! She looked happy and a much different dog to the curled up, near-to-death dog we'd met just a couple of hours earlier.

"Any blood?" I asked as Juliet bent down to give Sheba a stroke and some love.

"Just a couple of drips forming," she replied. "Nothing serious...yet."

Over the hours that followed we watched Sheba constantly as she tottered about on unsteady legs, the front ones so bowed we wondered if she'd ever be able to stand up straight. Our other dogs came and went, sometimes stopping to check her out, sometimes just passing her by, and ignoring her completely. This was, so far, the best introduction of a new dog to our pack we'd experienced. I'm truly convinced that the rest of the pack knew Sheba was special, that she'd gone through hell and needed time to recover from her terrible start in life. The vet who worked for the pound had put her age at under a year, maybe just a year at most and we'd see what our own vet said on Monday.

For the time being, however we had the rest of the weekend to get through. Clearly, Sheba was in no fit state to go for a walk, so, helped by Rebecca and Victoria, we took our dogs for their afternoon walks, making sure either Juliet or I was at home to watch over and care for Sheba at all times.

Walks completed, it was time for tea! We wondered how Sheba would react at feeding time. Having been starved for so long, we knew it wasn't the best idea to give her a full-sized meal. Her stomach and digestion system probably couldn't take it and it could even make her ill.

We decided to give her a small bowl, with maybe a third of what she should be receiving based on her size. We had a set routine at feeding time, with some dogs eating in the utility room, some in the kitchen, based on size and the speed at which they ate. We decided to feed Sheba separately, in the hallway, to give her the chance to eat without feeling threatened or being interrupted by the faster eaters.

All our dogs were fed on the same food, one which over the years we'd found suited them all and which they ate and enjoyed without leaving a scrap. Knowing Sheba had been starved we had to be careful that a change to a regular diet didn't cause her to suffer from any gastric or digestive problems, so we watched with great interest as we prepared the dog's dinners. Would she react positively to the prospect of food as our other dogs always did?

Having separated her, and with the others all fed, we turned to Sheba. She looked lost and forlorn as she sat trembling in the hallway, obviously wondering what was happening. Juliet placed the bowl of food in front of her and we waited to see if she'd eat any of the dried food mixed with a couple of forkfuls of dog meat. Individually and together, we quietly encouraged her to investigate the bowl that stood in front of her. At first, she seemed almost reluctant, or perhaps frightened to approach the bowl, but after I went down on one knee and gave her a loving stroke and spoke a few a few kind words to her, I took a piece of kibble in my hand and held it close to her nose so she could smell the food.

Sure enough, she sniffed at the solitary little piece of food and as I moved my hand to place it close to her mouth, she sniffed at it once more before exploring it by giving it a tiny lick.

"Come on, Sheba, it's nice. It's for you little girl."

In reply to my quiet urging Sheba eventually opened her mouth and took the food from my hand. I reached into the bowl and extracted a very small handful of the food, this time with some of the dog meat included and to my delight, Sheba took it from me and quickly devoured it.

"How's she doing?" Juliet asked from the kitchen where she was supervising the other dogs as they ate. She'd deliberately left me to it, not wanting to overwhelm Sheba or make a big deal of it and perhaps scare her away from the food.

"I think we're getting there," I replied and to confirm my words, Sheba's tail began to wag, slowly at first, and then a little faster, followed by her taking a step forward and dipping her head into the bowl. With her tail wagging even faster, the little dog now hungrily tucked in to her meal. Lisa at the pound had told us that despite her obvious hunger, Sheba had eaten very little while in their care. Like us, they'd fed her little and often, as you would a puppy, but it had only been in the last week she'd been with them that she'd begun to eat properly.

Now, with her confidence established, Sheba literally demolished the contents of the bowl within about a minute. She even licked round the empty bowl as if savouring the last lingering taste of the meal.

"Good girl, Sheba," I said as I fussed her and gave her a gentle hug. As tempting as it was to refill her bowl and let her eat more, I resisted the urge as it was important to introduce her to her new diet slowly and without placing a strain on her digestive system.

With some food in her tummy Sheba seemed to perk up considerably and she came to me and rubbed up against my leg in what could only be seen as a show of affection. We'd made a connection! We just had one problem to attend to in the aftermath of her first meal with us. All that tail wagging had set off the bleeding once again and though not as bad as before, there were quite a few blood spatters on the walls in the hallway and on the carpet, not to mention a few on my jeans.

Out came the medicated wipes and the towels again and we gradually stemmed the flow once again. Juliet was able to clean the blood from the walls and carpet by some fast work and we waited to see how Sheba would progress as the evening approached. Her arrival home had disrupted our usual dog walk-ing routine so we now took in turns to walk the dogs in short shifts, though it was obvious that Sheba was in no fit state for a walk yet.

She did however appear more receptive and lively than she'd appeared just a few short hours ago. A little love, some kind words, and a nice meal seemed to have worked wonders for her. She began to show more of an interest in her surroundings and as our other dogs became used to her presence, they began to approach her and investigate this new member of our family. Sheba retained a degree of nervousness as three or four of them gathered around her and I was a little apprehensive in case she thought they were about to attack her. Somehow, she must have sensed they meant her no harm as she simply sat on the kitchen floor as they looked at her for a minute or two and then walked away in ones and twos.

Both Juliet and I spent as much time as we could that first evening just re-assuring her and making her feel at home. Already, she seemed relaxed and comfortable with us. We were so pleased when, without any encouragement, she toddled across the kitchen floor and managed to climb into one of the dog beds and curled up and went to sleep. That was a great sign and we felt positive about the future for the little dog. Surely, we both believed, she wouldn't die in a few weeks. We both felt that all she needed was lots of love, some good veterinary care, good food and some much needed exercise and fun in her life, once she was well enough to enjoy it. Time would tell of course, but we now had hope for Sheba's future.

\* \* \*

Bedtime arrived before we knew it and Sheba, who'd slept most of the evening, would probably have been quite happy to be left in peace in her bed, but we realised she hadn't been out in the garden yet and so hadn't been to the toilet since arriving hours earlier. She was so sleepy that I had to pick her up and carry her out into the back garden, where to my surprise, she walked unsteadily, following our other dogs, and without further encouragement, proceeded to 'perform' as expected. I was delighted and made sure I gave her a love and lots of praise so she'd hopefully repeat the procedure in future.

We decided to see how she got on, sleeping in the kitchen with the rest of the dogs, rather than isolating her, where she could feel lonely and afraid. As she and the rest of the pack had behaved well together all afternoon and evening we saw no reason to expect trouble in the night and we were proved correct when we rose the next day to find Sheba curled up in bed, gently snoring, just where we'd left her the night before.

She looked up sleepily as I greeted her and all the dogs, and in an effort to start as I meant to go on, I put the kettle on to boil to make coffee for me and tea for Juliet, and then went and unlocked the back door, a signal to the dogs that it was time to get up. Most of them dutifully began to get out of their beds and made their way into the back garden where they could go to the toilet. Imagine my surprise and delight when little Sheba, her legs still quite weak, pulled herself out of her bed and followed the others. I in turn followed and watched her as again, she copied the pack and did both a wee and 'the other' as she'd done the night before.

She came back into the house and instantly made a bee-line for me, and gave me what I can only describe as a big 'doggie-kiss' on my leg, bare under my dressing gown. Her tail wagged as I made a fuss of her, and my first thought was, *Please, don't start bleeding again, not at this time of the morning.*

Greatly relieved to see no sign of blood, I finished making the tea and coffee and as per our normal routine, left the dogs to their own devices for a few minutes as I took the drinks up to our bedroom where Juliet was waiting to hear how things had gone for Sheba on her first night.

"She's fine," I told her. "Got up with the others and went out, did her business, came in and actually gave me a love and a kiss on my legs, then had a drink and got back into her bed."

"That's great," Juliet replied as she sipped her tea. "Let's drink up and go and see how she handles breakfast."

A few minutes later the two of us went downstairs and Juliet began preparing the dogs' breakfasts before making her own.

Sheba could hardly believe it, I think, when the feeding bowls were placed on the floor and she received another meal so soon after the one she'd eaten the previous evening. She must have thought she'd died and gone to doggy heaven.

She soon cleared her bowl, and we could already see a vast difference in her general demeanour and appearance.

She was too weak to join the others on their regular walks that day, but later, I managed to take her out for no more than ten minutes and she enjoyed a slow walk on her weakened legs, just up and down the road, but she loved it. She really enjoyed the feel of grass beneath her feet as we walked along the roadside verges, and was so happy that by the time we got home, she'd wagged her tail into another bleeding episode!

The rest of the day passed quickly and Sheba seemed to just naturally blend in with the rest of the pack, all of whom had instantly accepted her into their midst. Another short walk in the evening, and another good meal, still kept to a sensible amount, and the day quickly gave way to evening. This time, Sheba joined us in the lounge rather then sleeping the evening away in her bed. She soon found herself a place in front of the sofa and settled down, seeming to be intrigued by the sight and sound of the television. She'd obviously never seen one before and was quite hypnotised by the moving images she saw on the screen.

Bedtime came round all too soon, and after once again showing what a good dog she was in the garden, Sheba soon curled up in her bed, looking thin and emaciated, but, so much improved in the short time she'd been with us. The following day would be Monday and the vets would be open. I would phone and book Sheba in as soon as they opened. I knew when I explained the situation and circumstances, they'd see her right away. For now, it was lights-out time on Sheba's first full day with us. As we drifted off to sleep that night, Juliet and I shared a wish that the vets would give us a positive prognosis on Sheba's long-term health, as we both feared the possibility that her internal organs may have been adversely affected by the abuse and starvation to which she'd been subjected up to now in her life. Tomorrow would certainly be an important day for our Sheba.

## Chapter 3

# Sheba meets Bernard and … Rain!

Exactly as I expected, as soon as I explained about Sheba to the vet's receptionist first thing the next morning, I was told I could take her to the surgery right away. Our new little girl had spent another peaceful, relaxed evening, had slept well and with each meal she ate, we could see her strength gathering almost by the hour. The three weeks she'd spent in the care of the staff at the Dog Pound had obviously helped her to gain some weight, and perhaps it had been the loneliness of being isolated in that tiny pen that had contributed to her lethargy, as she now seemed very wide awake and gaining in energy. The staff at the Pound had of course done their best for her, but didn't have the time or the facilities to give her the round the clock attention we could. Just under two days in our home had brought about a vast improvement in her condition, as far as I could tell.

As I walked into the vet's surgery and the girls behind the reception desk saw Sheba toddling along beside me, they gasped. There were a couple of other clients and their dogs in the waiting room already and I couldn't help but notice their reaction to Sheba's appearance. I hoped they wouldn't think I was responsible for her terrible appearance.

"We just rescued her on Saturday," I said to the waiting room in general. "Poor dog was used as bait for training fighting dogs."

Those few words had the desired effect and one of the receptionists immediately came round to the front of the counter and went down on her knees to give Sheba a loving hug and stroke. Sheba loved it and wagged her tail, and guess what? Yes, her tail started bleeding again!

The two ladies waiting with their dogs made sympathetic noises, though I'm sure they'd never seen anything like it in their lives as Sheba wagged her tail with blood spatter being generously sprayed around the waiting area.

"Don't worry about it," the receptionist said. "At least the poor girl's happy. We'll get it cleaned up once you've gone in to see Bernard."

The second girl on the desk went and brought a mop and bucket while Sheba continued to receive lots of love and affection from her colleague and a minute later, Bernard, the vet, popped his head round the treatment room door and called us in. The receptionists would, I'm sure have explained to the waiting clients that emergency cases like Sheba took precedence over regular appointments.

Bernard, who had treated my dogs in the past, was absolutely terrific in his examination of Sheba.

"It looks like she's had a very hard life, Mr. Porter," he said, as he began his assessment of her condition, being gentle and caring towards Sheba who responded well to his gentle voice, allowing him to open her mouth and conduct a full physical examination.

He pointed out the fact that Sheba's chest appeared slightly concave, as though her breastbone hadn't developed properly as a result of malnutrition from an early age. Even now, ten years later, it's possible to see the slight deformity in her chest area. Her skeletal appearance caused him to voice his opinion on what should happen to people who treated animals in such a fashion and that surprised me, as I'd never known him to be an overly demonstrative person. Obviously, even vets have a limit on just how much animal abuse they can take!

As he continued his examination I asked him how old he thought Sheba was.

"It's difficult to be accurate because of her emaciated condition, but if forced to make a guess, I'd say she was between ten and twelve months old," he replied. "She's had a horrendous first year of life, Mr. Porter, but I'm glad you found her when you did."

I informed him of what the people at the Dog Pound had told me about her not being expected to live long. A look passed across his face that I saw as one of determination. I think I knew at that point that Bernard had decided that Sheba was going to be something of a 'project' for him, and I was right.

"I think we'd better do all we can to make sure that prognosis is an incorrect one," he said. "Certainly, she's going to need building up, and you'll have your work cut out in training her to be fully socialised after what she's been through, and we're going to have to do something about this tail of yours, young lady," he said to Sheba as he checked it over.

"Yes, she's obviously been trying to bite at it, probably as a result of starvation," he confirmed. "It's not in a great condition, I'm sad to say. I'll prescribe a gel for you to apply three times a day, and you absolutely must wear surgical gloves when applying it as it's very strong stuff. Make sure you wash your hands afterwards as well. It may take a month or two, and after that time, if it hasn't worked, we have to consider amputating the rear half of her tail."

Well, that was certainly telling it straight. I knew that we had about eight weeks to try and save Sheba's tail. I'd never seen, and definitely couldn't imagine a staffy with only half a tail, so I was determined from that moment, to make sure I applied the gel without missing a dose, to give the tail every chance to heal.

"Is there anything we can do to help her fur grow back, Bernard?" I asked.

"Her fur should grow back naturally in time," he assured me. "I take it you know why the dog fight people shave the bait dogs?"

"The people at the Pound explained it to me," I replied.

Bernard spent a minute or two reiterating the treatment to which Sheba had in all likelihood been subjected and it was easy for me to see he had strong views about the perpetrators of such acts. Then, having completed his initial examination of Sheba, he first of all gave her the first of her inoculations, necessary for all dogs, and which he was sure she wouldn't have been given in her past life. Next, he prescribed a medication that would help her body to fight off any infections as a result of the numerous sores on her skin plus a supplement to add to her food which would act to help to build her up to something like the proper weight for her age. He estimated that a dog of Sheba's age and breed should weigh around 12 – 14 kilograms. When we'd placed her on the scales in the surgery, Sheba just barely weighed SIX! She was just a kilo heavier than Cassie, out little Yorkshire Terrier/Australian Terrier crossbreed. It was evident to Bernard and to me, that we had a long way to go to bring Sheba back to full health.

Finally, Bernard checked her ears and found them to be full of dirt and debris. He set to work gently cleaning them out and it was almost unbelievable to see the horrible black grit and other detritus that came from her ears. Poor dog must have found it hard to hear with all that blocking her ear canals.

A short time later, Sheba and I left the surgery, armed with various medications, including antibiotics and cream for the sores on her body and a supply of surgical gloves that Bernard had given to me, to use when applying the gel to her tail.

\* \* \*

The next few days passed quickly, as Sheba grew a little more confident each day. Having said that, it has to be taken in context as, bearing in mind all she'd gone through, she remained a very nervous dog. At least, however, she had quickly learned her name and came to either one of us immediately if we called to her. In truth, I think she knew that coming to one of us meant she'd receive a love, a cuddle and perhaps a little dog treat for her efforts. I soon found that she enjoyed playing with a tennis ball and loved to lie on her tummy with one between her paws, playing with it, just as a cat plays with a ball of wool in similar fashion. Despite all she'd experienced in her shot life, she had at least retained her puppy-like instinct for play. I felt sure that once she was a little stronger and we could take her for regular, longer walks, she'd enjoy running and chasing the ball and bringing it back, I hoped.

Her settling in period was made so much easier by the fact that she quickly established a friendship with our pack leader at the time, Tilly, a highly intelligent Bedlington Terrier/Glenn of Imaal Terrier crossbreed, with a penchant for dog agility and a great sense of loyalty towards me. Despite her size, Tilly had a massive personality that allowed her to assert her authority over our other dogs by use of her body language more than anything else. She would walk beside Sheba on lead walks and would frequently touch her with her nose in a sign of reassurance. Those walks with Tilly may have been quite short in those early days, but they did wonders for Sheba's confidence.

Of course, there was still the matter of Sheba's tail. After Bernard had cleaned up the offending article in the surgery, we could see just how raw and damaged it was.

Apart from the bleeding and the obvious soreness, it appeared to be slightly bent near the end, and we wondered if, supposing we could save it from amputation, she would end up with a deformed tail with a distinct 'kink' in it. As for the gel we hoped would help her wounds to heal, this was an area where we soon found another reason to fall in love with our new little girl.

Each time I donned the surgical gloves and called her, Sheba obediently walked up to me, tail wagging, as if she knew what was about to happen. Sure enough, she stood still as I took hold of her tail in one hand and began applying the gel with the other.

It was as I applied the gel that both Juliet and I noticed the way she winced as the cream was spread on her tail.

"I think it must sting like mad," Juliet said when she first noticed Sheba screwing her face up as I smeared the gel on her tail.

"I bet it does. Bernard said it was powerful stuff, so it must feel like her tail's on fire. But it's as if she knows I'm trying to help her. She could easily have turned on me, if not aggressively, maybe just to give me a warning nip, but look how good she is."

Sure enough, every time I used the gel on her, Sheba would wince in obvious pain but never once did she show any sign of being aggressive. We'd built up an amazing bond of trust with the little dog in such a short space of time. She was loving her new life and enjoyed nothing more in the early days than playing with her tennis ball with me in the back garden. Meanwhile Juliet and I took it in turns to take her for short walks around the block, not wanting to let her mix with other dogs (apart from our own of course), until after she'd had her second injections, giving her full protection from common diseases and ailments.

During those walks, we both found ourselves fielding questions from passers-by or from people who knew us, as they saw us walking what they must have seen as a living skeleton along the paths near our home. Even though she was gaining weight quite quickly as a result of regular feeding and the medications she'd been given, poor Sheba still must have looked a shocking sight to those who saw her out with either one of us. Once we explained her history, people responded with a mixture of shock and sympathy. I think it would be fair to say that, like us, the majority of people, let's call them the man or woman in the street, were pretty much totally ignorant of dog-fighting and the type of people who indulged in this most cruel of activities.

My thoughts on it are quite simple. It can only be seen by any decent human being as a cruel, brutal and totally unnecessary activity, certainly not one that could in any way be thought of as a 'sport' as those who indulged in it tried to call it. How any sane person could want to force their own dogs to fight another dog, often to the death, is surely bad enough, but to use weak and innocent dogs as 'bait' to enhance the training of such dogs is, for me, the height of barbarity and cruelty. Since we'd adopted Sheba I'd made it my business to find out as much as I could about this appalling activity and had been further horrified when I learned there was, (and still is), a lucrative market in stolen pets, most of whom are destined to be used as bait dogs for these almost inhuman creatures who masquerade as dog owners while forcing their own and other people's dogs to participate in this brutal and barbaric act of what I see as the very height of dog abuse.

It must be heartbreaking in the first place for any loving pet owner to find that their dog has been stolen, but to then have to contemplate the possibility that their poor, much loved pet has ended up in the hands of the dog fighters must add such intolerable stress and grief to the original sense of loss. Some of the stories I learned as a result of my research were indeed enough to reduce a grown man to tears, and are really not appropriate reading matter for a book such as this, which may be read by younger people and children. Let's just say that anyone involved in dog fighting is below contempt and if discovered, should be prosecuted with the full force of the law. I'm pleased to say that the police in the U.K. take such cases seriously and do indeed prosecute those found to be involved in dog fighting rings, though by that time it's usually far too late to save many dogs that've fallen victim to those involved.

So, as I said before digressing, Sheba was doing well, gaining weight, albeit slowly and her tail, though still looking pretty ragged, was improving thanks to the 'magic gel' prescribed by Bernard, and we had high hopes for the future.

* * *

It was during her second week with us that we discovered we had a small problem. While walking Sheba one morning, and by now she was able to walk quite well for about twenty minutes, it began to rain. Sheba suddenly appeared very distressed and began pulling on her lead as though something had spooked her. Her face actually made me think she was in pain and it took very little time for me to realise what was causing the problem.

It had to be the rain. I knew instantly that because she had hardly any fur, and the sores on her body were still red and open, the rain on her back must be having a stinging effect on her. Luckily, we were only about five minutes from home on the return leg of our walk and I walked as fast as I could with her pulling me along, until we arrived home and she relaxed as soon as were in the house.

"Poor Sheba," Juliet said, as she gently patted her down with a dry towel. It wasn't possible to rub her down with the towel as that might have opened up some of the healing sores and made them bleed.

"It must feel like someone's pouring acid on her skin," I suggested. "You know how painful it is for us if we get into a bath with an open cut. That burns like hell. Poor little dog must have wondered what was happening when she felt the rain burning her sores out there."

Once she was warm and dry, Sheba ceased to panic and became her usual, lovable self again. We now knew she would have to be protected from the rain in future, at least until her coat grew back again. She already wore a very soft collar to prevent chafing her neck, where we'd found the remains of at least three old ligature marks, plus a still quite new one and we now considered buying her a nice dog coat to keep the rain off her while walking. Unfortunately, when we tried a couple of our other dogs' coats on her they also appeared to irritate her, obviously movement making them rub against the sores, and it was plain to see that until her fur grew back substantially, Sheba couldn't go out in the rain at all. We could only hope for a long, dry spell and that if it did rain, there'd be sufficient spells when the rain would let up enough to allow us to take her out, even for a very short time. Just in case, I took to carrying a large golf umbrella when walking her, so that if it did begin to rain, she'd have some protection until I could get her home again.

When I took her back to the vet for her second round of vaccinations, Bernard agreed that the rain probably did cause a burning or stinging sensation on her skin, but he was pleased with her progress and thought it wouldn't be too long before her fur grew back and he was especially pleased with the amount of healing already present on her tail.

We thought we were doing well with Sheba and that nothing could stop her from making a full recovery. I think I've mentioned that we made some mistakes along the Sheba's road to recovery. Luckily, most of them were of a minor nature, but, just when we believed everything was going well, things suddenly took a turn for the worse.

# Chapter 4

# Goodbye, Sheba

It began as a normal Sunday. We all got up at the usual time, the dogs all enjoyed their usual breakfast and as we took them for their usual morning walks, none of us could have envisaged the trauma that lay in wait for us just a few short hours away.

The other dogs had all had a great time running free on the nearby playing field, and Sheba had enjoyed her longest lead walk to date. Lunchtime came and went and, as was our usual routine on a Sunday afternoon, which we'd suspended for the three weeks Sheba had been with us, we decided to take a short trip to a nearby pub-restaurant, where children were allowed to accompany their parents. Juliet and I enjoyed this short break as a rule, being able to relax with a drink or two while the children could have a drink with us and run around and play in the gardens if they wanted to.

I found myself short of cash, so left everyone at home while I took a short trip in the car to the nearest ATM where I drew out some money for our Sunday afternoon trip out. As I pulled up outside our home, no more than ten minutes later, I still had no inkling of what was about to transpire.

All that changed as I walked through the back door to find Juliet in tears, cradling little Cassie in her arms, blood dripping from a wound, or wounds somewhere in the region of her front legs and shoulders. Not only was Cassie bleeding profusely but there was blood on the walls and carpet in the utility room. In fact, the utility room resembled a murder scene from a horror movie.

"What the hell's happened?" I blurted out, shocked by the sight that greeted me.

"It was Sheba," Juliet replied. "There was no warning. Everything was peaceful and she must have suddenly decided to attack Cassie for no reason. Look at the state of her."

I had to admit, Cassie looked terrible. Being a Yorkshire Terrier/Australian Terrier crossbreed, she was the smallest dog in the pack, not more than twelve inches long and weighing around four and a half kilograms, little more than two bags of sugar. With blood dripping from her wounds, and her coat matted and tangled with the blood that had already soaked her fur, it was hard to tell just how bad her injuries were.

"Something must have triggered it," I replied.

"But what?" Juliet cried. "As far as I know, Cassie did nothing to provoke Sheba."

"Where is Sheba now?"

"In the lounge. I managed to get her to let go and I just grabbed her collar and dragged her in there, out of the way," Juliet sobbed. "We can't keep her if she's going to start attacking the other dogs, Brian, she'll have to go back to the Pound, I'm sorry."

Much as I baulked at the prospect of returning her to the Dog Pound, Juliet's logic seemed sound at that moment.

"Where were the kids when it happened?" I asked as I tried to rationalise what had happened in those few short minutes I'd been away from home.

"Thankfully they were upstairs in their rooms, but they both came running downstairs when they heard all the commotion and Cassie squealing. They're in the lounge with Sheba now. Sheba seems just as traumatised as Cassie, to be honest."

I could think of no way out of the situation at that point, other than Juliet's assertion that we had to return Sheba to the Dog Pound.

"Maybe she'd be better off in a home with no other dogs," I said as I looked at Cassie, my heart heavy with sadness for her injuries and also for Sheba, for whom we'd had such hopes. After all, she was still recovering from the abuse and neglect she'd suffered and had been doing so well. It did make sense at that time, to let her go and maybe they could find her another home with a family that would love her and give her their undivided attention.

Without saying another word, but with a heavy heart, I pulled my mobile phone from my pocket and reluctantly dialled the number for the Pound. I was grateful to hear the friendly voice of Lisa when my call was answered.

"Lisa, we have a problem," I said, in an unwitting parody of the words associated with the ill-fated Apollo 13 moon mission.

"What's wrong, can we help?" Lisa replied, obviously able to tell from the tone of my voice that something was seriously wrong.

She listened sympathetically as I explained what had happened and I almost choked on the words as I finished by saying, "Can I bring her back to you? Juliet says we can't trust her and if she does something like this again she could kill one of our dogs if we're not around to stop her."

"Of course you can," Lisa said. "Don't worry. It's not your fault. I'm sure you've done all you can for her."

"Thanks Lisa. I'll be there within the hour," I said and hung up and turned to Juliet. "I'd better get going then. You can go and see to Cassie while I'm out and if it looks bad after you've cleaned her up, I'll have to take her to the emergency vet."

"Yes, okay, I'll take her up to the bathroom when you've gone. I'll be able to see better when I've used the shower to get rid of most of the blood."

I walked through to the lounge to find Sheba sitting peacefully in between Victoria's feet. She got up as soon as I entered the room and walked to me, her tail wagging. I felt awful, and in fact, I could virtually feel my heart beating in my chest at the thought of taking her away from the only home she'd ever known, but it had to be done.

"You've been a very naughty girl, Sheba," I scolded her and her tail fell as if she could tell I was angry with her. "I'm taking her back to the Pound girls. Your Mum and I can't risk her doing something like this again."

Both girls looked really upset and Victoria asked if she could come with me to say goodbye to Sheba. I agreed, feeling that her company would be more than welcome on what I knew would be a rather lonely journey home.

When I clipped her lead on, Sheba again wagged her tail, thinking she would be going for a walk, but the walk extended no further than the car, when I picked her up and loaded her into the rear compartment of our estate car. I'd remembered to pick up her medications before leaving the house, hoping the people at the Pound would make sure she took her medicine and that they'd apply the gel to her still healing tail.

When we arrived at the Pound, Lisa was ready and waiting for us.

"What will happen to her now, Lisa?" I asked.

"We'll do our best to rehome her, of course," she replied.

"She needs her tablets and her gel for her tail," I said. "Do you think you'll be able to give her her meds and see to her tail?"

"We will if we have time. You know how busy things can get round here."

"I know," I said feeling worse and worse by the second. If I was going to leave Sheba there, I had to go, as fast as I could.

When Lisa removed Sheba's collar and lead and placed a rope lead round her neck, I felt terrible. Poor Sheba dutifully walked away by her side until they reached the corner of one of the buildings that would take her out of sight. I looked round and Sheba was standing there, looking at me with pleading eyes that seemed to be saying, *Why are you leaving me here? What have I done? Don't you know I love you?*

Before I knew it, Lisa gave a little tug on her lead, and Sheba disappeared from our sight. I felt Victoria's hand suddenly take hold of mine and looked down and saw tears in her eyes. It took all my self-control not to join her in crying right there in the car park.

As we drove home in relative silence, I looked in my rear-view mirror and couldn't help seeing little seven-year old Victoria quietly sobbing on the back seat.

"Are you alright, Victoria?" I asked, already knowing the answer, but knowing what else to say.

"I'm going to miss Sheba," she sniffed in reply.

"I am too, sweetheart," I replied, "but you do understand why we had to take her back, don't you?"

"Yes, I know, but couldn't we have given her one more chance?"

"Perhaps, but what if she did it again and maybe ripped poor Cassie to pieces? You wouldn't want that to happen, would you?"

"No," was the one word answer that told me Victoria wasn't totally convinced by my argument, and, truth be told, neither was I.

"Don't forget, we might have to take poor Cassie to the emergency vet when we get home. It looked like her leg or her shoulder was badly hurt before we came out. We'll see how it looks after Mum's cleaned it up and had a good look at the wounds.

Victoria had fallen into silence and stayed that way for the remainder of our journey. We were soon home again and hurried into the house to see how Cassie was.

Juliet was waiting at the back door as we walked in, with Cassie in her arms.

"What's the verdict?" I asked her.

"Well, it's amazing really. She's not half as bad as I first thought. It obviously looked much worse then it really was. When I cleaned her up in the shower and had a really good look at the wound, it's not very big at all." She gently held Cassie's leg up to show me. There was a small bite mark in what we might term her 'armpit' where her leg joined her body at the shoulder. It was still bleeding a little bit but Juliet was mopping it up with a wet-wipe from time to time, to stop it dripping on the floor.

Juliet then looked at me and then at Victoria. She knew instantly that we were upset.

"What was it like when you took her back?" she asked.

"Awful, to be honest," I replied. "Sheba toddled off with Lisa but when she realised we weren't going with her she just stood still, staring at us, looking lost and alone. I felt like a mass murderer if you must know and Victoria was in tears, saying how much she'll miss her."

"Do you think she'll be okay?"

"I don't know. I don't even know for sure if they'll keep up with her medications."

"Well, at least Cassie looks as if she's going to be okay."

"She probably just needs some antibiotics to prevent infection. I'll take her to the vet tomorrow."

All of a sudden, we fell silent, as though neither of us knew what to do or say. We'd never faced a situation like this before and I'm sure we both wondered if we'd done the right thing. Obviously, Cassie's screams and the amount of blood she'd lost initially had given us a slightly inflated view of her injuries, but we'd acted with the best of intentions, and we'd have to live with our decision.

"Why don't we go to the pub as we planned?" Juliet eventually broke the silence. "It will do us good to get out of here, have a drink or two and then come home and walk the dogs."

"What about Cassie?"

"She'll be okay. She probably just needs to lie down and rest anyway."

"Okay," I agreed, and we all went upstairs to get changed for our now slightly delayed visit to the pub.

Half an hour later, we set off, all four of us still in a rather subdued state. What had begun as a normal everyday kind of day had turned into a pretty awful one and though it had never crossed our mind until a couple of hours ago, the decision had been made. Sheba was gone!

# Chapter 5

# Wrong Choices

The pub was warm, welcoming and filled with the usual hubbub that went with a crowded room populated by late Sunday dinner eaters, enjoying meals from the carvery, and an assortment of regulars and occasional visitors. The usual, middle-of-the-road piped music played at a comfortable volume in the background. I acted almost like an automaton at the bar, ordering my usual pint of Guinness, a white wine for Juliet and soft drinks and crisps for the kids. Somehow, being there didn't feel as relaxing and as good as it normally would have done.

As I sat at the table that Juliet and the girls had managed to secure for us, I was greeted by virtual silence apart from mumbled thanks. We sort of all sat staring into space for a minute or two before I broke the accompanying silence.

"I take it everyone's missing Sheba?"

"We are," Juliet replied. "I'm wondering if we were a little hasty in getting rid of her. We've been sitting here worrying about what might happen to her if they can't find anyone to adopt her. Plus, even if they do, will she get the care and attention she needs to recover properly and live a full and happy life?"

"I agree with everything you just said, but what can we do about it now. I've already taken her back and signed her over. And what about what she did to Cassie?"

"Maybe she just needs some special training. You could have a word with Brian Gallagher and see if he can suggest any ideas."

Brian was a canine behaviourist and trainer I'd worked with on some of our other dogs in the past and I knew if anyone could sort out any socialisation problems, he was the man.

"Maybe we should have discussed it more before rushing to take her back to the Pound," I said.

"It was my fault," Juliet said. "I just saw all the blood where she bit Cassie and thought it was far more serious than it really was. I should have waited until I'd cleaned her up before telling you to get rid of Sheba."

The children were sitting like statues as they listened to our conversation, until Victoria said, "Can't we get her back?"

Juliet added, "Yes, why don't you phone Lisa and see if they'll let us change our mind?"

I knew then that we all agreed. Returning Sheba to the Pound had been a very bad choice, not just for Sheba, but for the family too.

"I can try," I said, and without another word, I rose from the table, my Guinness still untouched, and walked outside, where I could make a phone call in peace.

"Lisa, it's me again," I said when her familiar voice answered my call. "We've had a family meeting, and we think we acted far too hastily in taking Sheba back to you. She deserves a second chance and if you don't mind, we'd like to give her that chance."

"Of course we don't mind," she replied.

"Thank God," I said. "I'm not sure how Juliet and the girls would have felt if you said no."

"We know you well enough by now," Lisa responded. "If you're willing to take her back, we know you'll do the best you can for her. We could all see what a difference the last few weeks with you have made to her since she was brought in to us originally."

"Thank you so much, Lisa. How soon can I come and get her?"

"It'll have to be tomorrow, I'm afraid. We're closing in about five minutes. There's no way you'll make it here by then, is there?"

"No, there isn't," I reluctantly agreed. "But I can be there as soon as you open at noon tomorrow."

Feeling greatly relieved, I walked back into the pub and quickly sat down opposite Juliet, reaching across and taking her hand in mine. The two girls sat waiting, expectantly.

"Well?" Juliet asked. "What did they say? Did you speak to Lisa, or was it Kay?"

"It was Lisa. She says it's okay for us to go and collect her tomorrow."

"That's such a relief," my wife replied and the two girls, Rebecca and Victoria both bounced up and down on their seats with excitement.

"Can't we get her back today?" Victoria asked.

"I'm sorry, but no, Victoria. The Pound closes any time now and we'd never get there in time. Don't worry, she'll be fine. It's only one night and then she'll be home with us again."

"But she'll be missing us, and her nice warm cosy bed, and her tea, and lying in the lounge with us all watching telly, and it's cold and horrible there," Victoria went on, making me feel even guiltier.

"I know she will, Victoria, but I'm sure she'll be okay and just think how excited she'll be when I turn up tomorrow to bring her home."

"What time are you picking her up?" Juliet asked.

"I'll be there when they open at noon," I replied. "Now that we've got it sorted, can we all try and cheer up a little and enjoy our drinks?"

Juliet squeezed my hand as she said, "Thank you," and I squeezed back. We knew we'd made a bad mistake and now we hoped we could correct it without it having had too much of a detrimental effect on Sheba.

"I'm also going to call Brian and make sure he's okay with me taking Sheba to a few training sessions," I said, referring to our friend the dog trainer.

"I still wish I knew what made her turn on Cassie like that," Juliet mused, trying her best to figure out just what had happened to cause such upheaval in the house just a short time ago.

"What were they doing at the time? Don't you remember?" I asked.

"Everything was the same as usual," Juliet replied. "The dogs weren't doing anything out of the ordinary, in fact, most of them were lounging in their beds when it all kicked off."

I could sense she was thinking of something and encouraged her to tell me what had sprung to mind. It could be important.

"Well, you know how Cassie loves to play?"

I nodded.

"What if she jumped on Sheba, trying to get her to play and her claws caught one of Sheba's sores or something like that? That would have been painful and Sheba's mind would have seen it as an attack, like when she was used as a bait dog."

"That would be typical, of Cassie," I replied. "That's probably what happened, though we'll never know for sure. We're just going to have to be extra vigilant until we know Sheba can be trusted not to do anything like it again. Brian will help to get her properly socialised."

When I made that particular statement, I was again forgetting the vast amount of abuse and trauma Sheba had been subjected to in her life so far. It was another minor error on my part, an assumption that we'd learn from in due course.

With the phone call made, arrangements in place to collect Sheba the following day, the atmosphere at our table lifted from one of gloom and despondency to one of hope and expectation. Whatever happened from that point onwards, Juliet and I knew we'd never let Sheba go again. Whatever it took, we were determined to make her life with us a happy one, and one in which she could become an integral part of our pack of rescue dogs. She'd done great up until that Sunday. There was no reason why she couldn't do even better once we brought her home again.

The girls were happy and talkative once more, and we all returned home from the pub to find Cassie full of life and vitality. The wound on her leg already looked so much better than it had when we'd left for the pub earlier. I said I'd still take her to the vet in the morning, just to be on the safe side, but I didn't think there was even need of any stitches to close the wound.

The rest of our dogs all seemed to realise there'd been trauma in the home and it was a relief to get them all taken out for their evening walks so they could release any built up tension by running around and playing on the field near our home. Tilly, however, seemed rather subdued. She, more than any of the dogs, was clearly missing Sheba, her new friend.

"Don't worry, Tills," I said, using my nickname for her, "Sheba's coming home tomorrow."

I always used to tell people that I was certain Tilly could understand English. Whether she truly could or not, I don't know, but I can say that after I said those words, Tilly began furiously wagging her tail. She, too, was happy at the news!

# Chapter 6

# Daddeeee!!!

The following morning dawned, bright and sunny, reflecting the overall mood in the house. Though we'd all missed Sheba the previous night, the feeling was tempered by the knowledge that I'd be collecting her and bringing her home again today.

First of all, however, I had to make a call to the vet to have Cassie's wound checked over. After we'd completed our early morning dog walks, I was in time to call the vets just after opening time. I had no trouble getting Cassie booked in and was given an appointment in just half an hour.

This time, instead of Bernard, I saw Rebecca, the practice manager, who at a future date would of course become Sasha's vet as those who've read her story will know. Cassie bounded in to the surgery, full of her usual unbridled energy and I almost felt a fraud for taking her in. With all the really sick dogs who must be in need of attention, here I was with this bundle of boundless joy who looked as fit as a fiddle. Outwardly, there was no sign of her wound and the way she kept leaping from the floor up on to my lap and down and up again made her look like a demented Jack-in-the-box!

Rebecca soon called us in though, much to my relief and I quickly gave her a run down on the previous day's events, leaving out the fact we'd taken Sheba back to the Pound. She'd be with us again shortly, so her status bore no relevance to Cassie's immediate treatment. Rebecca agreed that the wound wasn't serious, though it took her a while to get Cassie to stay still long enough for her to examine it. No stitches were required and Rebecca gave her an injection of antibiotics and prescribed a few days on Metacam as a painkiller. She laughed when I said to her, "Does she look in pain to you, Rebecca?"

"Not really," she smiled, "but we'd better be on the safe side. It might feel a little stiff in a day or so, so the Metacam will help her cope with any discomfort."

I took the opportunity to ask Rebecca if she thought Sheba's bite on Cassie could have been a fear reaction, and after I'd given her a quick resumé of Sheba's history, she agreed that my theory was probably correct.

"If Cassie was leaping around and jumping on her the way she's bouncing around in here this morning, it wouldn't surprise me at all if Sheba felt threatened and tried to defend herself," she said.

"We'll try and make sure Cassie doesn't get the chance to do it again until Sheba's fully socialised with the rest of the dogs," I told her.

"That's a good idea, Mr. Porter. We wouldn't want any harm coming to either of them. From what you've told me, Sheba still has some healing to do. Bernard's taking care of her isn't he?"

"Yes, he is, and Sheba's coming along really well."

"Good. So, this little one is fine and can go home. No need to bring her back unless you have any concerns. The wound should heal up in about a week to ten days. I know your wife was probably a little panicked by the bleeding you describe, but remember that dogs tend to bleed very profusely in comparison to humans."

"Thanks, I'll remember that in future."

With that, I left the surgery, Cassie bouncing along beside me and a bottle of Metacam in my pocket. The first stage of today's busy schedule was completed.

Juliet was relieved when we got home and I told her what Rebecca had said. We'd learned another lesson that morning and in future we'd remember that point about dogs bleeding rather more profusely than we do. It was information that over the years has stood us in good stead and prevented more than one unnecessary journey to the vets when a couple of our pets have sustained minor cuts and scratches. We already had the powder that helped to stop bleeding and we'd always use it whenever one of our dogs sustained such injuries. Almost without fail, the bleeding would soon cease and after cleaning up any wounds, we'd usually find them to be not worth troubling the vet with.

Next job that morning was to phone Brian, the dog trainer. After giving him the details about Sheba and the incident with Cassie, he told me she'd be welcome at his classes and told me she could start on Saturday. Brian was unfazed by the incident with Cassie and as usual, was confident in his ability to correct

Sheba's possible psychological problem in believing other dogs were going to attack her.

* * *

The morning flew by and before I knew it, the time had come for me to set off for the Dog Pound. Juliet asked if I wanted a bite to eat before leaving home, but I said I'd wait until I returned home with Sheba. The journey to the Pound normally took between 20 and 30 minutes, depending on the level of traffic, so I set off at 11.30, intending to be there just as they opened at noon.

My timing was perfect, and I pulled up in the car park at a couple minutes to twelve. The gates were still locked when I tried them but within a minute, Lisa arrived to open up.

"I take it you couldn't wait to get here," she laughed.

"You could say that," I replied. "How is she?"

"She's fine, don't worry. Once she sees you she'll probably just think she's been on a little overnight holiday. Let's go and do the paperwork again and then I'll go and get her for you."

"I'm sorry for messing you around, Lisa," I apologised.

"Listen you did what you thought was the right thing, and it's great you want to give her a second chance too, so don't apologise. I wish everyone who came here looking for a dog was as responsible as you and Juliet."

With that, we entered the office where the basic paperwork signing Sheba back over to us took only a minute. While Lisa went to fetch Sheba, I took her collar and lead from my pocket and waited at the same corner from which I'd walked away from her the previous day. A minute later, Lisa appeared at the corner of the building with Sheba walking submissively by her side. Lisa slipped the rope lead from around her neck and mouthed the words "Call her."

"Sheba, come here," was all I said and Sheba looked up, saw me standing waiting for her, and literally set off at full speed in my direction and ended her run with a leap in the air that took her into my arms. Thankfully, I caught her and was then subjected to a plethora of doggie kisses as she displayed her sheer joy and happiness at seeing me again.

Lisa was laughing and said, "I think that was her way of saying *Daddeeeee*. I think she's happy her Daddy's come back for her."

"I think you're right, Lisa," I laughed as well as I gently lowered Sheba to the ground where she stood wagging her tail with excitement.

"That's one of the nicest things I've ever seen," Lisa said. "That little dog obviously loves you so much and she's only been with you a few weeks."

"I know, that's what we worked out yesterday after I'd brought her back."

"I'm happy for her," Lisa replied as I walked towards her and shook her hand and said my thanks before turning and walking Sheba out of the gates, and soon had her settled in the car, after she'd actually tried to jump into the rear compartment. Sheba was going home…again!

I drove as fast as the speed limit would allow, keeping an eye on my rear view mirror, where I could see that Sheba was standing up, her paws resting on the bars of the dog grille, her head moving around as she took in the sights of the journey. Did she know where she was going? I'd like to think she did, and soon enough I pulled up outside our house, and as I exited the car, Juliet came walking down the path to meet us, having been watching for our arrival from the lounge window.

"Is she okay?" she asked, as I walked to the rear of the car to open the tailgate.

"See for yourself," I replied, lifting the tailgate, allowing a hugely excited little Staffy to leap from the car onto the road, jumping up and down, her front paws wrapping themselves around Juliet's legs in a loving grip, her tail wagging furiously.

"Sheba, hello again. Wow, anyone would think you'd been gone for a year. You're home now, baby," Juliet exclaimed as she tried to calm Sheba's delight and exuberance.

"You should have seen what she did at the Pound," I said, and went on to explain to Juliet about Sheba's leap into my arms when she saw me.

"Come on then, let's get you inside," Juliet said as we led Sheba down the path towards the back door. She'd deliberately left Tilly and a couple of the other dogs in the back garden so Sheba could be greeted by familiar faces as we walked through the gate. Sure enough, there was a great deal of tail wagging and sniffing each other as Sheba quickly became reunited with her doggy pals.

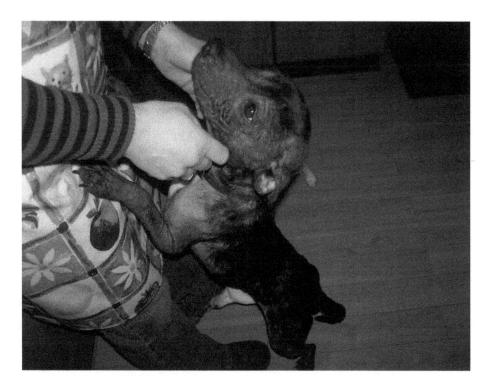

"It's going to be interesting to see how Cassie acts when she sees her," I said.

"Only one way to find out," Juliet said as she opened the back door and called the other dogs out into the garden.

They all came running out, some stopped to see Sheba, most just ran down the garden and carried on as if she wasn't there, including Cassie, who didn't seem to have any fear or trepidation when she realised Sheba was back. In fact, over the years, we've found Cassie to be one of the toughest and most dominant of our dogs, despite her miniscule size.

As our pack has developed over the years, we've realised that the other dogs are actually quite scared of little Cassie. I mention this in case anyone thinks Cassie is a tiny, 'victim in waiting', surrounded by bigger dogs just waiting to take chunks out of her. Not for nothing do we call her 'The Mad Ferret' or 'The Wicked Witch of the West'. She's like a Duracell Bunny without an off switch, and even now, at the age of twelve, she can run and run and run all day with no sign of fatigue. It can make you tired just watching her.

She also loves to hide under the coffee table in the lounge in the evening, or alternatively will 'perch' on the back of the sofa, from where she has a great position to survey the rest of the room. If any dog tries to disturb her while

under the table, she'll leap out at them like a Moray Eel striking from its un-
dersea hiding place, letting out a high-pitched screech, (not a bark), and it's
quite hilarious to see the Staffies, like Sheba, (really), Muttley and Sasha running into the centre of the room and rolling on their backs, legs in the air in
submission, or often running out of the room altogether. Those who encroach
on her space on the back of the sofa usually receive similar treatment. This tiny
terrier, (should that be 'terrierist?') is definitely no shrinking violet.

Likewise, out on the playing field, she is often the cause of great amusement,
where she is well known as an accomplished 'ball thief', often stealing another
dog's ball and running for all she's worth across the field, hotly pursued by
the ball's owner. Many a time we've had to chase her down to retrieve some
poor dog's ball after they've given up trying to catch up with her. Alternatively,
should another dog get too close to her personal space, or try to steal *her* ball,
Cassie is well known for seeing off the guilty party. It's quite hilarious to see
this tiny terrier chasing dogs as big as Rottweilers or Dobermans at top speed
across the field, their owners creased up with laughter at the sight. Oh, no, just
in case you thought she was a poor defenceless mite, this is one tough cookie.
Earlier this year, she needed an operation on a ruptured cruciate ligament. Six
weeks rest, the vet said! We couldn't stop her trying to run around on three
legs the night we brought her home after the operation!

But, time to return to Sheba's return. Not only was she totally excited and so happy to be home again, but the other dogs all seemed equally pleased to see her, especially Tilly and Sophie, our greyhound/lurcher cross. They both made a great fuss of Sheba and if we needed further confirmation that we'd done the right thing in bringing her back, it came when the girls arrived home from school and made such a fuss of Sheba, which she fully reciprocated, with much tail wagging, jumping up and down, and licking.

Sheba ate her meal with great gusto that evening and as a special treat I took her for a special walk, round the playing field where we hoped she'd soon be able to run and play like any normal dog. She loved it, and it was a shame I couldn't let her off to run and play with some of the other dogs we saw, but she wasn't ready for that just yet.

Time, and one or two more minor mistakes would teach us a couple of lessons in that respect but for now, we were in a happy time. Sheba was home again, and this time, Juliet and I vowed that this time would be forever. Whatever might go wrong in future, we'd deal with it, and with the right training, we'd turn Sheba into a 'real' family dog.

Chapter 7

# Training

The rest of the week saw no further negative incidents. Sheba continued to settle in well to her new home and new life. She began to put on weight and to our delight, we could see signs of her fur beginning to grow back. We could tell her coat had originally been brindle, with white on her chest. Her tail looked a lot better and a visit to the vet in the middle of the week for a check-up confirmed the improvement.

She was learning to play, a pleasure that had clearly been denied to her in her early life. Her tennis ball was her favourite toy and she loved nothing more than going with me to the playing field and playing 'fetch'. The wonderful thing about this is that I never had to teach her to bring the ball back to me. She'd run at full speed, pick it up and run back and deposit it at my feet and then look up at me as if to say, "Again, Dad." Of course, I complied and she made great use of her tail in displaying her happiness. It was a sheer joy to spend time with her, and her love and loyalty towards us was growing by the day.

Saturday arrived and I looked forward to taking Sheba to her first training session with Brian the dog trainer. Now is perhaps a good time to point out that the dogs that comprised our pack at the time of Sheba's arrival were not the same as those most people are familiar with today. Ten years is a long time, especially in the lives of our canine friends, so it's worth remembering some of those early friends of Sheba's. Many of them attended dog training sessions with her, but are sadly no longer with us. We all share fond and loving memories of Tilly and Sophie, who I've already mentioned, as well as Cairn Terrier Charlie, Molly the Westie, Snoopy our little crossbreed, and Chloe the Cavalier King Charles Spaniel. There were others over the years, some of whom only spent a short time with us, but, from the time of Sheba's arrival, only Dexter the Staffador, Penny the Jack Russell crossbreed and Dylan the Bedlington Terrier remain with us.

So, on that Saturday, Sheba would be accompanied to the training session by Tilly, who Brian tended to use as an example of what could be achieved at the sessions, and Charlie and Molly. The two girls, Rebecca and Victoria would accompany me to those sessions most Saturdays, as they enjoyed working with the dogs and today was no different.

Sheba's appearance proved a great talking point at the session that day and I found myself relating her short life history to at least half a dozen of the attendees. Brian was really good with Sheba and stuck to his usual methods, which included letting her off her lead for a short period of general socialisation. I told him I was a little worried in case she went for anyone's dog, but both he and his assistant, Carol, assured me they'd keep everything under control. They did, and it was good to see Sheba running around, with lots of other dogs she hadn't previously met, without her reacting aggressively towards them. I was still very wary whenever another dog got a bit too close to her, as I could see the fear in her eyes, but we managed to survive the session without mishap.

Afterwards, Brian told me he thought she was a great dog, but he agreed she had some issues regarding socialisation. Even though nothing bad had taken place that day, he, like me, had seen the potential in Sheba to react defensively if she perceived herself as being under threat. We still had a long way to go in making Sheba a socially acceptable member of the canine community.

Even so, I felt the first training session had gone well, and Brian agreed, especially when her background was taken into consideration. Over the next few weeks, Sheba learned more and more, her loyalty and obedience proved to be outstanding, and she would have everyone in fits of laughter when we had to do a long distance recall exercise. Carol would hold on to the dog's lead while the owner walked about 100 yards away, flanked on both sides by the other trainees, resembling a very long guard of honour, about ten yards across. The idea of the exercise was that the owner would call his or her dog when signalled by Brian and your dog had to 'run the gauntlet' through the avenue of dogs either side without deviating, and stopping when reaching it's owner.

Sheba would be 'champing at the bit' as Carol held on to her collar, and on Brian's signal I shouted, "Sheba, come!" and Carol released her. Without fail Sheba would run as fast as she could, straight as an arrow through the gauntlet of dogs, and as she got within about six feet of me, instead of slowing down and coming to a halt at my feet, instead, she'd literally launch herself into the air like a racehorse in the Grand National, trying her best to leap into my arms. Due to the speed at which she was travelling, however, as she hit my chest, it felt like I'd been struck by an incoming ballistic missile and although I did my best to catch her, the pair of us would invariable end up on the ground as I fell backwards, landing on my back with Sheba on top of me, licking my face for all she was worth, displaying a great big 'Staffy smile' as if to say, *"Aren't I a clever girl?"* accompanied by furious tail wagging.

Every week she'd do the same thing, and even though I was expecting it, it still came as a shock to the system to be bowled over by a ballistic staffy, much to the amusement of everyone at the training sessions.

"I don't think Sheba's quite got the hang of the word, 'stop', yet," Brian said one day, and that brought even more laughter from my fellow owners.

"I don't think she ever will, Brian," I replied with a huge grin. In fact, this behavioural trait led to Sheba developing what we might call her 'party-piece.' By standing still in front of her, and telling her to 'sit,' I found that if I said "Up,

Sheba," she would instantly perform a standing jump from the ground to my shoulder, wrapping herself around my neck and astounding everyone who saw her do it. Some of the other owners joked that she was the biggest parrot in the world, though it's no joke having a Staffordshire Bull Terrier perched on your shoulder like a demented parrot, I can assure you.

Another favourite exercise of Brian's was 'stealing your dog.' Either Brian or Carol would do their best to tempt your dog away from you by calling, offering treats etc. It was up to each owner to use their voice to control their dog, making them stay by their side. This was an important exercise as the incidences of dog theft were increasing locally and a dog easily tempted away from its owner would be a prime target for thieves.

Sheba seemed to take her cue from Tilly, who, despite any amount of calling and cajoling from the trainers, steadfastly stayed by my side as I repeatedly told her, "Stay." Brian was impressed. So was I, bearing in mind the short time Sheba had spent with us up until then.

The first training session had been a great success and we all went home happy and reported back to Juliet with Sheba earning lots of praise, and we received much tail wagging in return. Things looked good for Sheba, who had rapidly earned herself a place in our hearts. After such a terrible start in life, she was becoming a loyal, intelligent, and extremely loving little dog. Do dogs feel gratitude? It's a question we've often pondered over, and when we've looked at the bond that each of our rescues has forged with us, and considered how most were abused, abandoned or neglected, we've come to believe they do. The unconditional love each of our dogs has shown towards us, is a sure sign that they feel something like that, as they seem to appreciate and respond to their second, in some cases third, chance at a new life.

\* \* \*

As Sheba's health improved, we began to see a big difference in her appearance. Her fur had grown, and she now possessed a full, though still quite thin, brindle coat. The sores on her body had virtually all healed, with little or no scarring left to remind us of the pain and torture she'd previously been subjected to. The best news we'd had since she joined us came when Bernard the vet pronounced he was satisfied that her tail had healed. The 'magic' gel had done the trick, and there would be no need to perform an amputation of part of her tail. In addition, I could stop applying the gel, which Sheba had allowed me to smear on her tail, with great stoicism, despite the stinging effect it so clearly had on her.

Only one small incident marred those first weeks of Sheba's life with us. Again, it was all part of the big learning curve Juliet and I were experiencing as we coped with life with a severely abused and traumatised dog. As I've previously mentioned, Sheba's favourite toy at that time, (and today in fact), was a tennis ball and I'd spent many happy hours playing with her in the garden. Then came the day when I thought she was ready to take her ball on the playing field and really have some fun, with me having the opportunity to use a ball launcher to throw the tennis ball further than every before, so she could really stretch her legs while chasing it.

She'd already had a few sessions on the field, getting used to being around other dogs and learning that they weren't going to attack her. She'd even begun to make friends with the dogs belonging to a friend of mine, a German Shepherd and two small terriers.

So, there we were, all playing quite happily, and Sheba and the two terriers, together with Tilly and Charlie, were having fun chasing the ball. That is, until one of my friend's terriers got to the ball before Sheba and picked it up in her jaws. Before we knew what was happening, we heard a sharp squeal from the little dog and realised that Sheba had nipped or bitten her in retribution for having had the temerity to take Sheba's ball. On examining the terrier we found a small wound, something like Cassie's of a few weeks earlier, though not as severe.

My friend, knowing of Sheba's background, was very understanding and after she'd had her pet examined at the vet who gave the dog a painkilling injection and some antibiotics, I offered to pay the cost of the vet fees, and the matter was closed. This incident did teach us another lesson regarding Sheba's character and personality. Having come from such an abusive background, and never having had something as simple as a ball to call her own before, Sheba had become very territorial over the little yellow tennis ball and was simply not prepared to share her toy with any dog from outside her own pack, or family. She'd never exhibited this kind of behaviour at home, so we decided that, for now at least, we'd leave the ball at home.

Over a long period of time, we found it increasingly difficult to teach Sheba to be less possessive of her ball, so eventually, we found another, less well used field where we could take her and where few dogs could be found who might cause her to display any aggressive behaviour. We actually got into a great routine. I would take Sheba and maybe one more dog on a lead walk in the morning, and then, after school, Victoria would join me in taking her on the field, usually with Dexter, where she could play fetch with her ball to her heart's content. One of us could be her ball playing partner while the other could keep an eye on the entrance to the field and if we saw someone entering with another dog we could quickly end the ball game and put Sheba's lead on and carry on with a lead walk until either the other dog left the field, or the time came to go home. This arrangement served us well for a number of years, Victoria and I proving to be a great little team as she joined me in walking Tilly and her play friends who could all be allowed to run free quite safely as well as Sheba and Dexter, who is something of a couch potato and not really 'into' running around and exerting himself too much. He'd sometimes play with a stick for a few minutes, but would soon tire of it and return to sniffing around under the bushes that grew all round the four borders of the field.

Victoria actually grew so close to Sheba that she asked if Sheba could sleep in her bedroom at night. We agreed she could, as Sheba clearly idolised Victoria and so we moved Sheba's bed upstairs and until Victoria became a teenager and felt it a little 'uncool' to have a dog in her room, Sheba spent her nights with her. We'd often peek into Victoria's room last thing at night to find Sheba, not in her own dog bed, but snuggled up all nice and cosy on Victoria's bed, often snoring loudly, with Victoria blissfully sleeping in all ignorance of the sonorous droning.

So, after a 'false start,' Sheba's first year with us continued as she became perfectly 'at home' and settled in her new environment and when she'd been with us for about five or six months I entered a brief summary of her story so far plus a photograph of her into the monthly competition on a pet related website I subscribed to at that time. We were more than delighted when our former 'living skeleton' rescuedog won the 'Rescue Pet of the Month' award. It might not have been Best in Breed at Crufts, but it meant the world to us, on Sheba's behalf. She'd looked death in the face and survived and had made so much progress that she was in good enough shape to win this small accolade. Sheba was our little star!

**Rescue Pet of the Month**
June 2010

SHEBA
Animal Connection

27/04/20

Chapter 8

# Fear of Dogs, Love for People Young and Old

As happy as she was in her new home with us and our family of rescuedogs, Sheba gradually began to develop signs of nervousness when she was in close proximity to other dogs, not including her pack-mates at home of course. I noticed, while out walking with her, that she'd often begin to shake or tremble if she saw another dog approaching with its owner. One or twice, she'd even lunged at the other dog when passing, not a good sign, and one that made me think she was developing an aggressive streak.

"Quite the opposite," Brian the dog trainer assured me. "What it means is that Sheba's memories have imprinted certain fears in her mind. She was obviously used to being attacked by the fighters and now, she sees strange dogs as potential aggressors and is, in her mind, defending herself in advance. In other words, she's trying to stop them from attacking her by trying to strike first to tell them to go away."

I would never have thought of it like that, but when he'd fully explained it to me, I saw that what Brian was saying made a lot of sense. Sheba obviously proved that dogs have excellent memories and she had retained the fear that she'd lived with during her early life. Would she ever lose her fear? Time would tell, but Brian felt she would have difficulty in erasing those memories entirely. For now, Juliet and I did our best to try and instil confidence in Sheba. We tried introducing her to friend's dogs, on a one-to-one basis, but the trembling continued. She seemed okay at the training sessions, where Brian concluded she felt more secure in the company of her closest dog friends, Tilly and Charlie and also, rather oddly, felt less threatened in the presence of the large group of dogs that attended the training.

A friend has since suggested that maybe the 'bad men' as she calls them, only set one dog at a time on to her, so she feels less threatened within a group of dogs. Perhaps she also feels safe in the training group, knowing the humans there can be trusted not to harm her, but feels more threatened when out walking and encountering strangers, both canine and human, certainly a point worth considering.

At that point in time we could only show patience and hope Sheba would gradually overcome her fear. We knew it was early days for her. She'd gone through so much in her short life, and as far as we were concerned, she'd made great progress. After all, just a few short months ago, poor Sheba had been found, a living skeleton, a little dog with no name, lying on a rubbish tip, discarded, thrown away, and forgotten, like a piece of discarded garbage.

It was now almost a thing of wonder to see her proudly walking down the street with her tail wagging, her head held high, and a big 'staffy smile' on her face. Sheba seemed to find it easy to make friends with humans, even though she had a fear of other dogs. We found it quite remarkable that she reacted in such a loving way towards people she met on the street or on the playing field. After all, it was humans that had subjected her to the appalling abuse and torture she'd suffered in her previous life. Juliet and I both thought she would have been frightened of strangers, but instead, she showed just how wonderfully trusting and loving dogs can be. It made us think of her, tied or chained to a wall or post, in fear of the next attack by the fighting dogs, yet probably still wagging her tail and greeting her so-called owner every time they came near her, hoping to please them, looking for a little affection or a show of compassion. Pathetic as it may sound, it demonstrated just how wonderful a dog's feeling towards its owner can be. Hit them, scold them, abuse them and treat them like dirt, and a dog will still try its best to please its owner, and it makes the abuse and neglect of these loving animals all the more difficult to understand.

When out walking, if I stopped to talk with someone, Sheba's favourite ploy, if the person was friendly towards her, was to jump up and wrap her front paws round her 'victim,' mouth opening a big, wide staffy grin, and tail wagging at top speed. This would invariably bring Sheba lots of loving attention from even total strangers, who could hardly believe how friendly this dog they'd never met before could be.

Even more wonderful, though perhaps not too surprising, was the relationship that began to build up between Sheba and the local children. We'd often go for a walk in the afternoon, around the time when the infant and junior schools, full of 5 to 11 year-old children, were finishing lessons for the day. Sheba would wag her tail at some of the children and they, after their parents had sensibly asked if it was okay, would come to pet Sheba. My little dog would treat the children to a gentler version of her 'leg hugging' routine and soon, more and more children would stop on their way home to be given the 'Sheba treatment.' I think she did more positive work for the reputation of Staffordshire Bull Terriers than any advertising campaign could have done, during those walks among the schoolchildren.

Sheba has continued her love affair with children to this day and loves nothing more than being loved and petted by the smaller versions of the human race. Of course, over the years she's made friends with many adults too, none more so than two particular elderly gentlemen who live in our vicinity. She seems to love the elderly in the same way she loves children and one, named John, lives in sheltered bungalow accommodation nearby and would often say hello as we walked past his home on our walks. One day, Sheba 'insisted' on pulling me down his garden path to say hello back to him.

So began a long love affair between Sheba and John that continues to this day. John's wife often comes out to say hello too and has often joked, as John lovingly strokes Sheba behind her ears and speaks softly to her in loving tones, "It's been years since he's tickled me behind my ears or talked to me like that. I ought to be jealous." Every time we walk past his bungalow, if he's in the garden or sees us through the window, John comes out to see us and always says of Sheba: "She's my best girl. I love this little girl so much. I watch out for her every day and really miss her if I don't see you walking past." What a lovely tribute that is to Sheba.

Sheba's other special friend is Bert, another elderly gent who we'd see, usually on the return leg of our walk, as he made his way home from the pensioners Day Centre on his disability scooter. He'd always stop and say hello. He told me he'd always had a dog and owned a little Westie. He thought Sheba was adorable and she'd try and jump up on his scooter with him. He'd say, "Where's my kiss then?" and she'd climb up and give him a big, sloppy, Staffy kiss on the face and his couple of minutes of interaction with Sheba soon became a daily ritual and a highlight of his day, in his own words.

Jumping ahead to the current day, as I now walk Sheba with Sasha, the elderly folk in the sheltered accommodation bungalows often come out to see them both, especially on warm summer days, and they both receive plenty of impromptu treats from their little 'fan club' among the elderly residents. One lady recently said to me, "Until I got to know you and Sasha and Sheba, I would always cross the road if I saw a Staffy coming towards me. Now, I'm not afraid of them any more because I know what lovely dogs they really are."

So, Sheba, having left her awful beginnings behind, had become something of a local star, with her elderly 'fan club' and her ever-growing gang of mini-fans among the local schoolchildren. Her confidence was growing all the time, although, sadly, she still retained her fear of dogs outside of the home.

As time passed, we became resigned to the fact that Sheba would never fully feel at ease in the close presence of other dogs and we've come to accept it as part of her psychological make up and have made sure Sheba can live a happy life while keeping strange dogs at arms length. It certainly hasn't done anything to spoil her enjoyment of life.

Chapter 9

# Fireworks!

Having overcome so much in her fight back from a life of cruelty and abuse, life was pretty good for Sheba as winter crept up on us once again. The clocks had gone back an hour and most of the children in England were busily preparing for Bonfire Night, or, to give it it's correct title, Guy Fawkes Night.

For readers not familiar with this old English custom, allow me to explain. In 1605, Guy (Guido) Fawkes and a band of Catholic co-conspirators hatched a plot to assassinate the Protestant king of England, King James the First, in the hopes of restoring a Catholic monarchy to the country. Their plans involved exploding a large amount of barrels of gunpowder in the cellars of the House of Lords at a time when the King was scheduled to be present to address the members of parliament.

Unfortunately for Fawkes and his co-conspirators, they were betrayed by an anonymous letter to the authorities, Fawkes himself being caught red-handed, guarding the explosives. Fawkes was tortured and confessed the whole plot and sentenced to death. Somehow, he fell from the scaffold and broke his neck before the hangman's noose could do its work.

Ever since that time, The Gunpowder Plot as history has recorded it, has been commemorated each November 5th by the children of Britain by the lighting of bonfires, usually topped by a home made effigy representing Guy Fawkes and accompanied by fireworks amid a great party atmosphere. In my own younger days, we children would spend weeks collecting wood and other combustible material in order to create our back garden bonfires. Our mothers would sit for hours, sewing together our 'Guys' which we'd then wheel around the village in a wheelbarrow, knocking on doors and shouting "Penny for the Guy" when the householders opened the door. Depending on the quality of our effigies, we would usually be rewarded with a few pennies or sometimes more, all of which we'd save towards the purchase of fireworks for the big night. So, enough of history and my own childhood years, let's get back to Sheba.

Nowadays, as fireworks have become bigger, louder and more 'explosive' in nature, children can no longer walk into the corner shop and buy one or two at a time, as we used to, until we had enough for a good display. Now, only adults can purchase them and Bonfire Night, has to some extent, become something of a nightmare for dog owners and indeed for the owners of pets in general, made worse by irresponsible people who begin letting them off two or three weeks early and continue for a week or so after the date. There's currently a campaign in progress in an attempt to have fireworks limited to organised public displays.

The sound of modern fireworks exploding in the air and the concussive effect produced by the explosions can only be described as being something like being stuck in the middle of a war zone whilst under a mortar attack!

* * *

Now, quite remarkably, a lot of animals take the bangs and screeches of the night in their stride, but others, like Sheba and Dexter, find Bonfire Night absolutely terrifying. From that first November with us, we've had to cope with Sheba virtually turning to jelly at the sound of fireworks going off. She would run and try to hide under a table or a chair, or even under my, or Juliet's legs. Her fear was and still is something extremely pitiful to witness. Not just fireworks, but any unusually loud 'banging' noises cause such a terrible reaction in her. Over the years we've tried various calming agents, none of which had much affect although, recently we have discovered a product called Magicalm which, while not entirely curing her of her fear, does appear to have something of a calming effect on her, though she continues to shake and tremble, just not quite so violently. Dexter, the second of our 'firework fear' dogs, has never reacted quite as badly as Sheba but will also try to hide when fireworks begin exploding, and runs to us for reassurance when hiding doesn't help. The Magicalm tablets have had a far more positive effect on him than they have on Sheba, so their success is quite obviously linked to the level of the dog's fear in the first place.

Sheba's fear of loud noises and of fireworks in particular is just another part of her psychological make up and one I think she shares with thousands of dogs around the world. We always ensure we have sufficient Magicalm tablets in the house, not only for Bonfire Night, but in readiness for New Year's Eve, which, over the last few years has fallen victim to the 'curse of the fireworks,' something that has only grown in popularity in recent years. We can never know when someone will decide to have a birthday party and have fireworks as part of their celebrations. Only when action is taken to restrict their use, will the situation improve.

# Chapter 10

# Changes and New Arrivals

With Sheba fully integrated into our family, life took on a calm and peaceful routine, if coping with the needs of a large number of dogs on a daily basis can actually be called 'routine.' It's a sad fact that, over the years the names of those within our pack have changed, and we retain such wonderful loving memories of those who have shared our lives over the years.

Perhaps the change that affected Sheba most took place about six years ago, when Juliet and I returned from one of our visits to the Dog Pound with a tiny little white and black Staffy puppy who'd been found abandoned in a street gutter, almost dead from hypothermia. Sasha was about to enter her life!

From the very beginning, Sheba took to Sasha, befriending the little puppy who'd suddenly appeared in our lives. She'd follow her around the house and paid her great attention as Sasha gradually found her way around her new home, constantly exploring her new environment, her little tail wagging constantly. I think Sheba found Sasha's tail fascinating, as it was so tiny it resembled a little wriggly worm wagging away at the rear of her body. They made quite a picture at that time. Sheba was of course fully grown, and Sasha, having been abandoned long before she should have been parted from her mother, was very undersized, so much so that we'd had to buy her a little blue cat collar with a little bell on it, as we couldn't find a dog collar small enough to fit her.

It would have been natural to assume that Sasha would be the one doing the following, but it seemed more as if Sheba was fascinated by the miniature black and white version of herself that had suddenly appeared in our home. Wherever baby Sasha wandered during her early explorative days in the house, Sheba wouldn't be far behind.

"Do you think it's the bell that's attracting her?" Juliet asked one day, referring to the little bell that hung from Sasha's cat collar.

"Maybe it is," I said. "Whatever it is, something about Sasha has definitely got Sheba's attention. Maybe Sheba feels maternal towards her."

"I'm not sure about that," Juliet said. "If anything, Sheba seems to be the one who's doing the following, and if she was being maternal, it would be the other way round, surely."

"You're right," I agreed. "Well, at least they're good friends."

Within three short weeks however, that friendship was put on hold when Sasha had the accident that saw her break her leg for the first time. Playing upstairs with Dinky, and despite a baby gate across the top of the stairs to keep her safe while I was in the bathroom, our tiny puppy somehow fell through a crack between the banister rail and the landing floor and broke the elbow joint in her right front leg. Sasha had to have an operation to rebuild the joint and spent the next three months in a crate in the kitchen, with me sat beside her in a collapsible garden chair. Only allowed at to go to the toilet or for a cuddle with the family in the evenings, it was a long twelve weeks before she was given the all clear, and poor Sheba couldn't seem to understand why her new little friend couldn't come out of the crate to play with her. Sheba would pace around the kitchen, stopping frequently next to the crate where Sasha would look at her, wagging her tail, as Sheba looked increasingly confused.

Sheba seemed as pleased as the rest of us when Sasha was given the all-clear to return to normal life at the end of a very long three months, only for her to break the same leg again two weeks later, while attempting to jump over the baby gate separating the kitchen from the utility room. Another operation and three months 'imprisonment' in the crate followed and finally, having virtually 'lost' six months of her first year, Sasha again received the all-clear from the vet and she could again return to normal activities. During both of Sasha's long periods of rest and recuperation in the dog crate that became her virtual home for six months, Sheba was never far away, and would often be found, either sitting or 'standing guard' beside Sasha's crate, as though she was making sure her little friend was okay and also providing her with much needed canine company.

By now, Sheba had developed a real affinity with Sasha and it soon became clear that Sasha felt the same and the two dogs would spend many hours play-ing together and curling up to one another for short naps during the day. They were the best of friends and that was good for Sheba. Although she and Tilly were close, by the time Sheba had gained her health and strength again, she'd outgrown Tilly who would often come off worst in their little play fights. De-spite being much smaller than Sheba, Sasha was a little 'toughie' and could easily hold her own during 'rough and tumble' games with Sheba.

By the time Sasha was fully grown, it was clear to us just how undersized Sheba was. Due to the starvation and other abuse she'd suffered in her first year, her growth had been stunted and when Sasha was eighteen months old, she was quite a bit longer, taller and heavier than Sheba. We now also realised that the friendship between the two staffies had evolved into something more. Sheba had grown more and more dependent on Sasha, so we had a situation where the older dog now looked to the younger one for leadership and guidance. It was an early sign, though we didn't know it then, of just how much Sasha gives to those around her, both canines and humans.

* * *

This chapter is titled 'Changes' and I'm not going to go into the details of how we lost certain very loved members of our pack over the years, but when we lost Tilly, the pack 'dynamic' shifted dramatically. Whereas little Tilly had enforced her pack leadership through force of will and canine body language, it now looked as though we didn't have a new pack leader among the dogs, who all simply looked to me as 'top dog' for some time. We expected one of the other dogs would eventually assume some sort of authority over the pack, but it never happened. As a result, Sheba's reliance on Sasha became even more important. Sheba may have been much older than Sasha, but she was very much reliant on Sasha for much of her confidence. With Tilly gone, Sasha did step up to become the dog closest to me in terms of affection and it was another step in Sasha showing us her incredible capacity for empathy and love. With my 'special' dog gone, Sasha had decided to step up and take her place, so I suppose it's fair to say she became leader of the pack at that point, second only to the 'top dog,' me!

With Sasha in her second year and with more changes within the pack, Sheba found herself having to get used to more new friends. Most significant perhaps, was the arrival of the three puppies, Petal and Muffin and their brother Digby. We had lost one of our dogs and Juliet was in a state of depression for a while. I said we should look for a new puppy to give her something to focus on. I thought a puppy rather then a new rescue would be good for her as it would need more looking after from the beginning. We saw an advertisement in the local paper for Staffy cross puppies for sale. After a phone call we made a ten minute journey the next day to see the puppies, half Staffy and half Springer Spaniel.

Of the five pups, the owners of the Mum and Dad had decided to keep one which was a little runt and their son was going to have one. So we had a choice of three. We couldn't decide between the two bitches, one nearly all black with a white chest and one black and white. I left the final choice to Juliet, who decided on the little black one.

At home that evening, Juliet suddenly decided she was unsure of her choice. "Do you think I picked the right one?" she asked as we sat watching TV.

"There's no right or wrong one," I replied. "They were all gorgeous. All puppies are. If you want to change your mind, just say so. I'm sure they won't mind."

After thinking it over, she finally decided to stick with her original choice. Next morning, we were ready for our new arrival. I'd arranged to collect the puppy at ten a.m. and after having spent a long time thinking in the night, I waited until Juliet had taken some of our dogs for their morning walk and then phoned the puppies' owners. Without telling Juliet, I arranged a big surprise for her. I wouldn't be collecting the little black puppy that morning. I'd be collecting her *and* her sister!

Juliet could hardly believe her eyes, when, a couple of hours later, I walked into our house with a tiny puppy under each arm. She was overjoyed and we soon decided on names for our two new little girls. The black one would be Muffin and the black and white one would be named Petal, because the black markings on her back resembled the petals on a flower.

The puppies soon settled in, even more so when Sasha decided to become their surrogate mother. We were amazed to suddenly find Sasha proudly sitting in bed with them both, as they slept curled up at her feet. She'd decided to adopt a couple of babies!

The one concern we had as Sasha spent so much time with the new pups, sleeping with them, playing with them, going into the garden when they went out to play or go to the toilet, was how Sheba would react. As Sheba had become so attached to Sasha, would she become jealous of the puppies and become aggressive towards them? We needn't have worried. Once she realised what Sasha was doing, and probably recognising the puppies as being young and vulnerable, she decided she would help Sasha in taking care of the puppies. Before we knew it, the two puppies not only had a surrogate Mum in the form of Sasha, but they now seemed to have acquired 'Aunty Sheba' as well.

It was quite amusing to see this new little 'family' as Sasha would proudly lead the two puppies around, both of them obediently following her wagging tail, with Sheba dutifully bringing up the rear, as if watching their backs. This little procession would take place many times a day and as well as giving us cause for laughter, it was also very touching, showing without a doubt, that dogs have feelings and a sense of social responsibility within their own hierarchy.

A couple of weeks after we'd bought Petal and Muffin, we received a phone call from the breeders who offered us the last of the litter, a male dog, at a giveaway price. Apparently the man had taken the little pup to a home where the people wished to buy it, but took one look at the place and turned round and took the puppy home. No way did he think it a suitable home for a puppy. Thank God for responsible breeders. The lady told me they could tell how much we loved dogs when we'd gone to buy the two girls and they'd love us to take this last little one. What could we say?

I set off right away, and within an hour, I returned home with our latest family member, who we named Digby. His sisters were delighted to see their sibling again, and as for Sasha and Sheba, they took the new arrival in their stride and he quickly joined the regular 'puppy processions' led by 'Mummy Sasha.'

Even now, four years after their arrival, Muffin and Petal love snuggling up in bed with Sasha. Probably because he arrived a couple of weeks later, Digby was always a little more independent and has grown to be something of a 'Mummy's boy' and is very much Juliet's special dog. He does still sometimes manage a 'sneaky' cuddle with Sasha or Sheba though, so lovely to see.

Even with the arrival of the puppies, Sheba still retained her own special relationship with Sasha. It really was something special to realise that Sheba had become such a wonderful loving dog since those nervous early days as she fought her way back to health, and that she had found a way of adding a little of the missing confidence in her life by way of her ever growing dependence on the much younger, bouncy and exuberant Sasha!

# Chapter 11

# Terms of Endearment

Sheba was now over five years old and we'd had many opportunities to observe her at play, at rest and in every possible everyday situation. As such, we'd come to recognise many traits that served to reinforce her position as a much loved member of our family.

Perhaps the most obvious was Sheba's distinctive 'waddle' as she walks. Other Staffy owners might know this from their own dog's behaviour, though I've only seen one other dog do this, coincidentally another brindle staffy that lives nearby and is almost Sheba's double, apart from being a boy!

When she walks, Sheba has a kind of 'rolling' gait, that makes it look like she's waddling from side to side, with her tail held in what's best described as a 'pump handle' shape, like an old-fashioned 'S' shaped handle on a water pump. It's quite comical to watch as she trundles along beside Sasha, who walks with a distinct spring in her step.

When she sits waiting for her tea to be served in an evening, Sheba also does what we call her 'dinner dance, as she sits rocking from side to side, her front paws barely leaving the floor and her tail wagging in excitement.

As for preparing to go for a walk, Sheba will run into the utility room where the leads are kept, and will sit perfectly, with one paw in the air, ready to 'shake paws' before I attach her lead on to her collar. I have to go through the little ritual each time we go for a walk, and it's another cute example of her nature. When she wants a cuddle, she will also come to me or Juliet, offering her paw in her own way of asking for a love. After shaking her paw she then jumps up onto my, or Juliet's lap, ready for a cosy cuddle.

All these little things simply help to illustrate her loving and playful nature. Of course, her playtime with her tennis ball is perhaps her 'pièce de résistance' as she runs and jumps to catch her ball and automatically brings it back, drops it at my feet and patiently waits for me to throw it again. The great thing about this game of 'fetch' is that nobody taught her to bring the ball back, or to drop it and wait. Whether she learned this by watching Tilly or one of other dogs in her early days with us, I don't know for sure, but it's another terrific example of the intelligence of the breed.

As for grooming time, well, this is possibly Sheba's favourite time of the week. She absolutely loves it when Juliet lifts her onto the grooming table and begins her weekly session with the grooming brush. She adores the feel of the brush gliding through her fur and as Juliet moves to brush her under her chin, down her neck and chest she lifts her head high into the air, shuts her eyes and goes into 'doggy ecstasy' as she enjoys the massaging sensations the brush gives her.

This is a good place for me to tell you about 'Sheba's song.' One day, when Victoria was walking Sheba, Tilly and Charlie with me, we'd just finished playing on the field with them, when the heavens seemed to open up, without warning. The rain positively pelted down, massive raindrops literally bouncing up from the pavements and road surfaces. Deep puddles formed in seconds and Victoria and I, with three very soggy doggies, ran for cover. A nearby bus stop provided the only shelter around, so, even though it was wholly inadequate, being open at the front and sides, we did the best we could to avoid the worst of the downpour, though we were already soaked to the skin.

As we shivered and sheltered, waiting for the summer downpour to relent, Victoria and I began to amuse ourselves by making up silly songs. Victoria was about nine years old at the time, so Sheba would have been about four or five. Why, I don't know, but we decided to make up a song for Sheba. After a few minutes, with the rain continuing its relentless assault, we completed our little ditty,

To the tune of the old 1984 novelty pop song 'Agadoo' we now sang;

*Shebadoo, doo, doo, she's a staffy with a smile,*
*Shebadoo, doo, doo, she's been with us for a while.*
*She can bark, she can growl, and she likes to wag her tail,*
*But when she jumps up on your knee it's like being jumped on by a whale!*

Silly, maybe, but it helped alleviate the boredom of standing under that bus shelter as we waited for a let up in the downpour. Soon after, the rain stopped as suddenly as it had started and we made a dash for home, before the clouds could return to open up above us once again. As it was summertime, we soon dried off and warmed up after a change of clothes and when Victoria and I performed our song for Juliet she couldn't help giggling. That little ditty seemed to stay in our heads and when we took Sheba out to play on the field, we'd often sing it to her as walked along. Perhaps because the song contained her name twice in quick succession, Sheba seemed to realise it was especially for her and she'd proudly strut along the street as Victoria and I sang her little song to her.

I should explain that the 'Shebadoo' nickname had appeared sometime in Sheba's second year with us. Neither Juliet nor I can remember how it came about or who first used it, but the name stuck and was even extended to 'Mrs. Doos,' pronounced 'Dooz.' So, over time, Sheba has learned to respond not only to her real name, but will also come running if we call for 'Mrs. Doos' or simply 'Doos.' The variety of names certainly doesn't confuse her and she seems quite happy to be a dog with multiple names.

* * *

While we were learning all these things about Sheba's character, life of course went on as normal around us. Sasha of course, had gone through a tough start in life too, having suffered two leg breaks in her first year, and being diagnosed with skin allergies not long before the puppies entered our lives. Worse was to come however when, at just two and half years of age, Sasha contracted canine epilepsy.

Poor Sasha's life literally changed overnight, as she went from a happy, carefree young dog to one whose life depends on her taking a constant cocktail of medications to try to control the terrible seizures she suffers. Sheba soon realised things were different when she first witnessed her in the grip of a seizure and in her own way, seemed to be trying to encourage her to get up. You can read Sasha's full life story in my best selling book, *Sasha, A very special Dog Tale of a very special Epi-Dog*, available in Kindle and paperback editions from Amazon around the world.

In a way, we'd been fortunate that Sasha's first few seizures had taken place when she was separated from the rest of the dogs, as we now discovered that Sheba's idea of 'helping' Sasha was to nip at her as she thrashed around on the floor in the grip of the seizure. Digby unfortunately reacted in a similar way, and if we hadn't moved quickly to pull them away, Sasha could have ended up in quite a bloody mess.

After that incident we changed the routine of the home to accommodate Sasha's illness. From now, she'd spend her time almost exclusively with me in the lounge, where I spend most of my working time, and where little Cassie and Penny would stay too during the day to provide her with some canine company.

She'd still join the others at mealtimes, and enjoy walks with Sheba as usual, and be with us all in the lounge in the evening when both Juliet and I would both be present to quickly separate her from the others if a seizure occurred.

This arrangement has worked well over time, with only one 'slip up' when she went into a seizure while eating and Digby nipped her a couple of times. It's obvious also that Digby and Sheba are both frightened if Sasha collapses into a fit and they mean no real aggression towards her.

This brings me to Sheba's method of 'talking' to us. When she comes to one of us wanting something, whether it's a treat, or to go out in the garden, or just wants a cuddle, she actually 'communicates' with us by making what we call her little 'piggy' noises, a series of grunts that do indeed make her sound like a little pig. She's done this for many years now, and when Sasha has recovered from a seizure, she will actually go to her and make these noises, as if she is somehow 'talking' to Sasha. Whether she is or not, we'll never know of course, but wouldn't it be nice to think she's using some kind of canine language to 'talk' to her friend when she's unwell?

# Chapter 12

# Poison!

What has surprised us more than anything is Sheba's health over the years. We fully expected to be making fairly regular visits to the vet when we first took Sheba into our home and into our hearts. Yet, once her tail had healed in those first few months, and as she'd slowly gained weight, Sheba became an extremely healthy and robust dog. Apart from her annual visit to the vet for her booster vaccination, she never needed veterinary treatment for anything until one day, when she was six years old. One spring morning, we woke as normal and all the dogs, Sheba included, greeted us with enthusiasm as always. When their breakfasts were laid out in their bowls however, we noticed that Sheba wasn't eating.

"I've never known Sheba to leave her food," Juliet said, as she cleared the empty bowls away. "Do you think she's unwell?"

"I don't know," I replied and I called Sheba to me. She'd retreated to her bed, which was unusual, as she'd usually want to go out in the garden after breakfast. Sheba responded, slowly, and came to me, her tail between her legs. She looked decidedly poorly, her eyes had lost their sparkle and she seemed lethargic.

"I think you're right," I said to Juliet. "She's definitely not herself"

When, a short time later she refused to leave her bed to go for her morning walk, which she always enjoyed, I knew for sure that Sheba was ill. Why, and with what, I'd no idea. I'd been a dog owner long enough to know the difference between a simple case of diarrhoea, (starve them for 24 hours, plenty to drink, etc), and something more serious.

We both knew a visit to the vet was required when Sheba began shaking and then began vomiting profusely. She looked awful, and I had a feeling we had a very sick dog on our hands. A phone call to the surgery resulted in me being asked to take Sheba in right away. When we arrived, we were quickly ushered in to see Rebecca. I soon learned why.

"Come in, Mr. Porter, and let's take a look at Sheba. Unfortunately, we've had a few cases like this in the last few days. If I'm right, Sheba may have been poisoned."

"Poisoned?" I was taken aback by her words.

"Yes, a few other veterinary practices have also reported similar cases."

"But how, Rebecca?"

"We're not sure yet, but let's take a look at Sheba first."

Rebecca spent five minutes conducting a thorough examination of my poorly dog, only to confirm what she's thought. Sheba had a very high temperature, her tummy was extremely sensitive to touch, and all her symptoms added up to the fact she was suffering from some form of poisoning.

"Has she been playing or running on any open spaces or fields in the last few days?" Rebecca asked.

"Yes, she's been playing ball on the playing field where we usually go," I replied.

"We suspect someone, either singly or in a gang, are going round regular dog walking areas and laying poisoned food down, probably dog treats or pieces of meat, in bushes or park borders, etc, where dogs usually forage around when off their leads. The police are aware of it and there'll be an announcement in the local press this week."

"But, will Sheba be okay?" I asked, worry etched on my face.

"Thankfully, you've brought her in straight away, so we should be able to counteract whatever it is they've used. If only we had a sample of whatever she's bringing up, it would be a big help."

Right on cue, Sheba began to gag, and then promptly vomited all over the treatment room floor. Far from being displeased, Rebecca smiled and said, "Well done, Sheba. Now we have something to work with."

It was the first time I'd seen anyone who was actually happy to see a dog being sick on their floor! Together with a nurse, Rebecca took a sample of the vomit using a pooper scooper and the nurse then cleared the remainder with a mop and brush and lots of liquid disinfectant.

"We'll have the results of the lab tests later today," Rebecca told me. I knew our vets had their own in-house laboratory so they could act quickly in such matters. I left the surgery a few minutes later, after Sheba had received a pain killing injection, and armed with probiotics and other medications to help her stomach to settle down and recover.

Later that day, Rebecca phoned me.

"Sheba was definitely poisoned Mr. Porter," she said. "The lab tests showed a mixture of chemicals in her system, all of which point to the use of some household cleaning products. There are obviously some dog hating people out there, and the police have been informed and are investigating. Please, be very careful where you allow your dogs to run free until these people are caught and stopped."

"Don't worry; we'll be keeping them off the field for a while. Let's hope the police can find these idiots before long."

"At least we know what it is now. Can you call into the surgery and pick up another med for Sheba? Take one a day, plus use what I gave her this morning and she should be okay in a few days. Just starve her tonight and then she can have something to eat tomorrow, but just something bland, maybe a bit of chicken and rice or scrambled eggs."

"Okay, and thank you," I said and quickly set off to pick up the new medicine for Sheba. Poor dog still looked terrible, and had been sick twice more since seeing Rebecca that morning. By late evening however, she'd perked up a little as a result of the medications, and we felt a little more positive about her condition.

* * *

It took about a week for Sheba to return to full health again. It was a worrying first couple of days, as the shaking and lethargy that had affected her still remained for at least twenty four hours. After that, she did at least begin a slow but gradual improvement.

After the story of dog poisoning in the area was featured in the local press that week, the police did in fact soon make a number of arrests. We never did hear what made the small gang of dog-haters embark on their dangerous and cruel campaign, but it must have caused a great deal of heartache to many local dog owners, some of whom were not as lucky as we were with Sheba.

Sheba had lost quite a bit of weight in the week she was poorly, and it was surprising just how quickly she began to assume that emaciated appearance we'd seen when we first met her. Thankfully, once she started eating properly once again, she gradually filled out once again, and was soon back to what for Sheba was her normal weight.

Why anyone could harbour such hatred towards our canine friends I will never understand. I'm aware that not every person in the world shares my love of dogs, but nothing justifies such cowardly and cruel attacks on innocent pets and their families.

Sheba herself was soon enjoying life once again, running and playing and chasing her ball, displaying her big staffy smile for all to see in a display of her total happiness. As we returned to our normal walking routine, it was so touching to see her friends come out to see her. They all knew she'd been ill, having seen me walking past their homes with the other dogs, and Sheba simply lapped up the attention as her special friends in the sheltered accommodation in particular made such a fuss of her, giving her and Sasha treats and lots of love and cuddles, their pleasure at her recovery clearly displayed.

Her schoolchildren friends had obviously missed her and ran to greet her the first time I walked her at school closing time. Sheba loved the attention, and it was great to see her fully recovered from what was close to being another close encounter with death. If we hadn't acted promptly when she was first taken ill, it might have been too late for the vets to save her, but that doesn't bear thinking about.

When I see her with the children, it really makes me so proud of her. Staffies do have a wholly undeserved reputation at times, thanks to those who, over the years, have used them as 'weapon dogs' or status symbols of some kind, as if to illustrate how tough they are. Sheba is so loving and gentle with them, and yet, even today, I have to admit there are still some parents who, despite seeing how she behaves with her little 'fan club' of children, will drag their own offspring across the road to avoid going near her, or worse still, pull their kids past in a hurry when their little ones try to come and join their friends in making a fuss of Sheba.

"Come away," or, "Don't go near it," or "Leave it alone," are just some of the comments I've heard from totally uninformed and ignorant parents who are only succeeding in imprinting negative thoughts on their children and probably making them afraid of dogs for life, with no good reason. I've seen lots of children trying to hide behind their parents, or even worse, screaming in panic when they see a dog, any dog, not just a staffy, walking towards them. What way is that to bring up a child? As children, I and my friends all used to love to play with the neighbourhood dogs, apart from the rare few we knew that weren't particularly friendly. I think the world has moved too far into a 'cotton wool' culture, where parents try to cocoon their children from many activities or normal interactions with the world around them. To make a child afraid of all dogs purely through a parent's own prejudices is definitely not healthy, in my own opinion.

Of course, none of this meant anything to Sheba, who was simply happy to be fit and well again and back doing the thing she loves the most. We were very careful in the coming weeks to ensure our dogs didn't roam far from us when we eventually allowed them to run and play on the field again. Only when it was announced by the local council that all areas where dogs had suffered from any form of poisoning had been visited, checked and given the 'all-clear' by environmental health officers did people once again gradually regain their confidence to allow their dogs to use the playing field freely once again.

For Sheba, I'm pleased to say that was the one and only time we've had any health issues with her in the ten years she's been with us; quite remarkable given her terrible start in life. She is, indeed a very happy, but also a very tough and resilient little staffy.

Chapter 13

# Ageing Gracefully

As I sit writing this chapter, it's just over a week before Christmas, 2016 and I'm reminded that in a couple of weeks it will be the tenth anniversary of the day we travelled to the Dog Pound and found that poor, skeletal little dog curled up in a cold barn under a heat lamp.

So, not only will Sheba have been with us for a full ten years, but as she was already about a year old when we adopted her, it means she's now eleven and entering her twelfth year, a remarkable achievement for that very sick dog who wasn't expected to live very long when we loaded her into the car, took her home and found a luggage compartment full of blood on our arrival home. It all seems so long ago, and Sheba has had such a great life since we brought her home.

It would be nice to go back to the Dog Pound and tell them about Sheba, and how her life has panned out since that day, but the place is no longer under the same ownership, the staff who were there ten years ago are all gone, and I think it would terrify Sheba to death if we took her through those gates again. She really has a remarkable memory and would probably think we were going to leave her there again.

Going back to Sheba, it really is strange to think we've had her all this time, and yet she's still just as bouncy, happy and full of life as she was right after we'd helped her to return to full health. She still loves to run and play with her ball, and will walk for hours if given the opportunity to go on a nice long trek. The only noticeable difference in her is that we suddenly noticed this year just how grey Sheba has turned around her face. It's funny really; she must have slowly been turning grey but because we see her every day and to us, she's always the same old Sheba, we never really noticed it until now. Our little girl is rapidly turning into the canine equivalent of a silver-haired old lady, though I doubt any silver-haired old ladies would be ready to leap up onto my shoulder or run at full speed across a field in pursuit of a bouncing yellow tennis ball!

One rather 'spooky' occurrence happened very recently when a new lady moved into a house on the corner of our street, a mother with two young children, the youngest just coming up to three years old. The two little girls, both instantly fell in love with Sasha and Sheba when they met us out walking one morning soon after they'd moved in. Over the next couple of weeks, the two girls would run to make a fuss of my two dogs whenever they saw us, and the youngest girl became very closely attached to both Sasha and Sheba very quickly and the two dogs loved the attention they received from this very young, but very dog-friendly young lady, whose name I soon learned from her Mum. Sasha and Sheba's latest best friend is…Tilly! What a strange coincidence.

As she enters her twelfth year of life, she has proved to us and everyone who knows her just how rewarding it can be if a person takes the time and has the compassion to look into the possibilities of adopting a rescue dog. The fun and the enjoyment we, as a family, have been rewarded with since Sheba came into our family have more than outweighed the difficulties we faced when she first entered our lives.

She still adores Victoria, and though she may not sleep in her room or go for walks with her now that Victoria has entered the transition from teenager to young adult, the bond between them is as strong as it was when Sheba was to be found snuggled up in Victoria's bed instead of being in her own cosy dog bed in Victoria's room.

Most of all, it's her unique friendship with Sasha which is so touching to see. Sheba literally dotes on Sasha and depends upon her for her own confidence and self-assurance.

After mealtime in the evening, the two of them get together in the lounge and spend about half an hour playing together. They go through what we call their quite comical 'synchronised roly-poly' routine, when, oblivious to the other dogs in the room, the pair of them roll on their backs together, paws in the air, having a great time and even managing to play fight in their most ungainly upside-down positions. They quite simply take over the room as the others sit or lie watching their performance. On rare occasions they might be joined by Petal or Muttley, but it's usual for just the two of them to monopolise the lounge carpet until they've tired themselves out.

Thankfully, Sheba shows no sign of slowing down and is well able to keep up with the much younger Sasha, now just past her sixth birthday. To see the two of them running along, side by side, despite Sasha's back leg mobility problems and Sheba's age, is a joy to behold. With Sheba being so much smaller than Sasha, she also has to run a little bit faster to keep up, due to her having shorter legs! I love watching them run together, as they even manage to 'play fight' on the run, every so often turning to each other and trying to grab one another's snouts, (totally playful of course), and making little snorting noises; just so funny and rewarding to watch these 'best friends forever.'

Chapter 14

# The End of the Beginning

The beauty of writing a book like this is that it has no defined ending. Sheba will hopefully be with us for many years to come and I'd like to think she'll live to a grand old age. Given the start she had in life, I think it would be the very least she deserves, having shown such resilience and fortitude in recovering from the terrible cruelty and abuse she suffered when only a puppy. The people who treated her in such a deplorable manner truly robbed this beautiful dog of her puppyhood. When she should have been running and playing with puppies her own age, instead she was tied or chained up, her fur shaved off, living a life of constant fear as the fighting dogs were trained to use her as 'target practice.'

So, I think it's true to say that her story is really the end of the beginning, a beginning that commenced on the day she was first rescued, little more than a barely living skeleton, from a rubbish tip by a concerned dog warden, carried on during three weeks of care at the Dog Pound, and really got into gear from the day we found her and brought her home.

It's a beginning that saw her learn to be a member of a family and to live with and interact with a pack of dogs that she realised didn't mean her any harm. She needed medical care, which was provided by expert vets who cared about her and were determined to see her live a full and healthy life and she then responded to a course of training that helped her learn the basics of social behaviour.

Sheba, in many ways, epitomises what it means to be a rescue dog, given a second chance at life. Though she may not be 'perfect,' as in her fear reaction to strange dogs, she is, in every other way, a fully rehabilitated, loving family dog. The fact she has so many human friends of all ages, but in particular the very young and the elderly, speaks volumes for her appeal across generations.

I forgot to mention earlier that Sheba also has a very important 'job' within the pack. It's been very educational over the years to watch how a pack of dogs interacts and behaves as a social unit. The domestic dog, *Canis lupus familiaris*, owes many of its instincts and behavioural traits to its ancestor, the wolf, *Canis lupus*. Anyone who owns and lives with more than one dog is, in effect, co-existing with a mini wolf pack of their own. The pack seems to organise itself, so each dog has a role in the set-up.

As I was saying, Sheba has a very special job within the pack. You might think that with ten dogs in the house, we would be subjected to a cacophony of barking when someone knocks on the door, or when we admit a stranger to our home. That's not the case, however, as Sheba has been given the task of being 'chief of security' within the pack. She will bark when there's a knock at the door, and is sometimes given a degree of back-up by Muffin, who has obviously assumed the role of her deputy. Amusingly, little Cassie and Penny sometimes add a few high pitched 'woofs' but they would find it difficult to terrify or deter a rampaging earwig!

Sheba, on the other hand, possesses a strong bark and certainly leaves no-body under any illusions that there's a suitably 'qualified' guard dog in the home. Even Muffin's 'back-up bark' isn't really on a par with Sheba's, but she likes to think she's helping, I'm sure.

The rest of the dogs don't make a sound and just go on with what they're doing, whether it's sleeping, playing, or chewing a bone. Sasha seems to be the top dog, who somehow sends her orders to the rest of the pack, through body language and attitude. Digby is the 'youth leader' who seems to orchestrate playtime among the younger dogs, and Dylan has, for a long time, been in charge of protecting the back garden from the occasional foray by the neigh-bourhood cats. He's often found sitting, like a statue, in a corner of the garden, keeping a close watch on his territory, guarding the two bird tables, and will zoom into action if any feline decides to attempt an unauthorised entry into his domain, barking and chasing them away.

A sign beside our front door bears the words, 'Our staffies can reach the gate in two seconds, can you?' together with a picture of a staffy head. Any intruder would certainly think twice before breaking in, (though our lot are so 'brave' the worst they'd experience would probably be a severe licking). So it's a good job Sheba has a bark that should deter any burglar or other criminally-minded person.

So, as I said as this final chapter opened, this is certainly not the end of Sheba's story, but it is the end of the beginning. Her life is now a happy one, she has no reason to feel afraid of being abused or hurt; she has a warm cosy bed to sleep in, and is well fed, twice a day. She is loved and cared for by a family of both humans and dogs, and gets plenty of opportunities to play and be herself, and goes for two walks every day, whatever the weather.

With Sasha to keep her company on her walks, she is always close to her best friend, and she is always ready to receive lots of strokes and cuddles from me, Juliet and her wide circle of human friends in the local community.

Apart from the terrible start she experienced in her life, and the one case of random poisoning from which, thankfully, she recovered, she's been a fit and healthy dog for the last ten years. Her big 'staffy smile' will no doubt be a source of joy and pleasure for years to come, and her story, like that of Sasha's will go on for a long time to come.

Maybe, in time, some of her pack mates may find their stories appearing in print, but for now, Sheba, Sasha and all our dogs wish you all a Happy 2017 as the New Year approaches. It will be long after the holiday before you read this, but our wish is sincere and applies whenever you find yourself obtaining your copy of the book. It's been quite an emotional journey, recalling some of the worst times in Sheba's life but also a joy to recall the fun we've had with our beautiful rescue dog over the years.

Sheba would, I'm sure, want me to thank you for taking the time to read her story, and we both hope you'll maybe come and see her and our other dogs, all of whom make regular appearances on Sasha's own Facebook page, *Sasha the wagging tail of England* at

https://www.facebook.com/groups/270003923193039/

If she could add a closing message to what is, after all, her story, I'm certain that Sheba would ask you all to consider adopting a rescue dog the next time you're thinking of adding a dog to your family. They really do make the most amazing, loving, pets you can imagine. And as for Sheba's last word, it can only possibly be… *"Woof."*

# Acknowledgements

To all the vets and staff at Vets 4 Pets, I have to say a big thank you. Without the initial care and attention you lavished on Sheba ten years ago when I first took her into the surgery, I would never have been able to contemplate writing this book, because her story could have been a very short and tragic one.

Most recently, his amazing true life story of Sasha became a UK bestseller as well as entering the bestselling Top Ten charts in France, Canada and Australia. Shortly before going to print, Sasha won the Best Nonfiction Book Award in the Preditors and Editors Readers Poll Awards 2016.

As always, my thanks go to my friend and Beta Reader, Debbie Poole, who does her best to keep my writing on the straight and narrow, eliminating my many errors along the way, chapter by chapter, and to Miika Hanilla at Creativia Publishing, himself a dog lover and great supporter of my rescue dog book.

A big thank you must go to the many readers of *Sasha*, who, having read the chapter which told of her close friendship with Sheba, wrote to me and asked me to write Sheba's story in full. This book is my response to those many entreaties.

As always, my thanks go to my chief critic and greatest supporter, my dear wife Juliet who deserves such great praise for her daily efforts in walking most of our dogs, and for tireless work in grooming them so they always look their best,

Finally, I have to say a word in gratitude to everyone involved in dog rescue, everywhere. Without their continuing efforts, there would be fewer dogs saved from lives of terror and abuse or neglect. They deserve a medal, every one of them.

# About the Author

Brian L Porter is an award-winning author, whose books have also regularly topped the Amazon Best Selling charts. Writing as Brian, he has won a Best Author Award, and his thrillers have picked up Best Thriller and Best Mystery Awards. His short story collection *After Armageddon* recently achieved Amazon Bestseller status and his moving collection of remembrance poetry, *Lest We Forget*, is also an Amazon best seller

Writing as Harry Porter his children's books have achieved three bestselling rankings on Amazon in the USA and UK.

In addition, his third incarnation as romantic poet Juan Pablo Jalisco has brought international recognition with his collected works, *Of Aztecs and Conquistadors* topping the bestselling charts in the USA, UK and Canada.

Brian lives with his wife, children and of course, Sasha and the rest of his wonderful pack of ten rescued dogs.

He is also the in-house screenwriter for ThunderBall Films, (L.A.), for whom he is also a co-producer on a number of their current movie projects.

*A Mersey Killing and the following books in his Mersey Mystery series* have already been optioned for adaptation as a TV series, in addition to his other novels, all of which have been signed by ThunderBall Films in a movie franchise deal.

# Other Books by the Author

**Dog Rescue**

- Sasha - A very special Dog Tale of a very special Epi-Dog (Amazon best-seller)

**Thrillers by Brian L Porter**

- A Study in Red - The Secret Journal of Jack the Ripper
- Legacy of the Ripper
- Requiem for the Ripper
- Pestilence
- Purple Death
- Behind Closed Doors
- Avenue of the Dead
- The Nemesis Cell
- Kiss of Life
- **The Mersey Mystery Series**
- A Mersey Killing
- All Saints, Murder on the Mersey
- A Mersey Maiden

- (Coming soon) – A Mersey Mariner

- (Coming soon) – A Very Mersey Murder

- (Coming soon) – Last Train to Lime Street

- (Coming soon) – A Mersey Ferry Tale

## Short Story Collections

- After Armageddon (Amazon bestseller)

- (Coming soon) – A Meeting of Minds, co-author, Carole Gill

## Remembrance Poetry

- Lest We Forget (Amazon bestseller)

## Children's books as Harry Porter

- Wolf (Amazon bestseller)

- Alistair the Alligator, (Illustrated by Sharon Lewis) (Amazon bestseller)

- Charlie the Caterpillar (Illustrated by Bonnie Pelton) (Amazon bestseller)

## Coming soon

- Tilly's Tale

- Dylan's Tale

- Hazel the Honeybee, Saving the World, (Illustrated by Bonnie Pelton)

- Percy the Pigeon, (Illustrated by Sharon Lewis)

## As Juan Pablo Jalisco

- Of Aztecs and Conquistadors (Amazon bestseller)

Lightning Source UK Ltd.
Milton Keynes UK
UKHW010634271020
372315UK00001B/99